CIMA Exam Practice Kit

Fundamentals of Management Accounting

CIMA Exam Practice Kit

CIMA Certificate in Business Accounting

Fundamentals of Management Accounting

Walter Allan

Amsterdam • Boston • Heidelberg • London • New York • Oxford
Paris • San Diego • San Francisco • Singapore • Sydney • Tokyo

ELSEVIER

CIMA Publishing is an imprint of Elsevier
The Boulevard, Langford Lane, Kidlington, Oxford, OX5 1GB, UK
30 Corporate Drive, Suite 400, Burlington, MA 01803, USA

First edition 2008

Copyright © 2010 Elsevier Ltd. All rights reserved

No part of this publication may be reproduced, stored in a retrieval system
or transmitted in any form or by any means electronic, mechanical, photocopying,
recording or otherwise without the prior written permission of the publisher

Permissions may be sought directly from Elsevier's Science and Technology Rights
Department in Oxford, UK: phone: (+44) (0) 1865 843830; fax: (+44) (0) 1865 853333;
e-mail: permissions@elsevier.com. Alternatively you can submit your request online by
visiting the Elsevier web site at http://elsevier.com/locate/permissions, and selecting
Obtaining permission to use Elsevier material

Notice
No responsibility is assumed by the publisher for any injury and/or damage to persons
or property as a matter of products liability, negligence or otherwise, or from any use
or operation of any methods, products, instructions or ideas contained in the material
herein.

British Library Cataloguing in Publication Data
A catalogue record for this book is available from the British Library

ISBN: 978-1-85617-778-8

For information on all CIMA Publishing
visit our web site at www.books.elsevier.com

Printed and bound in Great Britain

10 11 12   10 9 8 7 6 5 4 3 2 1

Working together to grow
libraries in developing countries

www.elsevier.com | www.bookaid.org | www.sabre.org

ELSEVIER   BOOK AID International   Sabre Foundation

Contents

About the Author	viii
Syllabus Guidance, Learning Objectives and Verbs	ix
Examination Techniques	xvii

1 Cost Behaviour — 1
   Concepts and definitions questions — 3
   Concepts and definitions solutions — 5
   Multiple choice questions — 7
   Multiple choice solutions — 9

2 Accounting for the Value of Inventories — 11
   Concepts and definitions questions — 13
   Concepts and definitions solutions — 14
   Multiple choice questions — 16
   Multiple choice solutions — 18

3 Overhead Costs: Allocation, Apportionment and Absorption — 21
   Concepts and definitions questions — 23
   Concepts and definitions solutions — 25
   Multiple choice questions — 27
   Multiple choice solutions — 29

4 Cost–Volume–Profit Analysis — 31
   Concepts and definitions questions — 33
   Concepts and definitions solutions — 35
   Multiple choice questions — 37
   Multiple choice solutions — 40

5 Standard Costs — 43
   Concepts and definitions questions — 45
   Concepts and definitions solutions — 47
   Multiple choice questions — 49
   Multiple choice solutions — 51

6 Variance Analysis — 53
- Concepts and definitions questions — 55
- Concepts and definitions solutions — 57
- Multiple choice questions — 59
- Multiple choice solutions — 61

7 Cost Book-keeping — 63
- Concepts and definitions questions — 65
- Concepts and definitions solutions — 68
- Multiple choice questions — 73
- Multiple choice solutions — 76

8 Job and Batch Costing — 79
- Concepts and definitions questions — 81
- Concepts and definitions solutions — 83
- Multiple choice questions — 85
- Multiple choice solutions — 88

9 Contract Costing — 91
- Concepts and definitions questions — 93
- Concepts and definitions solutions — 95
- Multiple choice questions — 98
- Multiple choice solutions — 100

10 Process Costing — 103
- Concepts and definitions questions — 105
- Concepts and definitions solutions — 107
- Multiple choice questions — 110
- Multiple choice solutions — 113

11 Managerial Reports in a Service Organisation — 117
- Concepts and definitions questions — 119
- Concepts and definitions solutions — 121
- Multiple choice questions — 123
- Multiple choice solutions — 126

12 Functional Budgets — 129
- Concepts and definitions questions — 131
- Concepts and definitions solutions — 133
- Multiple choice questions — 135
- Multiple choice solutions — 137

13 Cash Budgets — 139
- Concepts and definitions questions — 141
- Concepts and definitions solutions — 143
- Multiple choice questions — 145
- Multiple choice solutions — 148

14 Flexible Budgets	**151**
Concepts and definitions questions	153
Concepts and definitions solutions	154
Multiple choice questions	155
Multiple choice solutions	157
Mock Assessments 1, 2 and 3	**159**

About the Author

Walter Allan has lectured, written, examined and published in the fields of Management and Accounting for the past 25 years. He has lectured on CIMA courses for a number of UK private colleges and is a former CIMA examiner. He is chief executive of Galashiels Economic Consultancy, a company which specialises in professional Accountancy training.

Syllabus Guidance, Learning Objectives and Verbs

A The Certificate in Business Accounting

The Certificate introduces you to management accounting and gives you the basics of accounting and business. There are five subject areas, which are all tested by computer-based assessment (CBA). The five papers are:

- Fundamentals of Management Accounting
- Fundamentals of Financial Accounting
- Fundamentals of Business Mathematics
- Fundamentals of Business Economics
- Fundamentals of Ethics, Corporate Governance and Business Law

The Certificate is both a qualification in its own right and an entry route to the next stage in CIMA's examination structure.

The examination structure after the Certificate comprises:

- Managerial Level
- Strategic Level
- Test of Professional Competence in Management Accounting (an exam based on a case study).

This examination structure includes more advanced papers in Management Accounting. It is therefore very important that you work hard at Fundamentals of Management Accounting, not only because it is part of the Certificate, but also as a platform for more advanced studies. It is thus an important step in becoming a qualified member of the Chartered Institute of Management Accountants.

B Aims of the syllabus

The aims of the syllabus are

- to provide for the Institute, together with the practical experience requirements, an adequate basis for assuring society that those admitted to membership are competent to act as management accountants for entities, whether in manufacturing, commercial or service organisations, in the public or private sectors of the economy;

x Syllabus Guidance, Learning Objectives and Verbs

- to enable the Institute to examine whether prospective members have an adequate knowledge, understanding and mastery of the stated body of knowledge and skills;
- to complement the Institute's practical experience and skills development requirements.

C Study weightings

A percentage weighting is shown against each topic in the syllabus. This is intended as a guide to the proportion of study time each topic requires.

All topics in the syllabus must be studied, since any single examination question may examine more than one topic, or carry a higher proportion of marks than the percentage study time suggested.

The weightings *do not* specify the number of marks that will be allocated to topics in the examination.

D Learning outcomes

Each topic within the syllabus contains a list of learning outcomes, which should be read in conjunction with the knowledge content for the syllabus. A learning outcome has two main purposes:

1 to define the skill or ability that a well-prepared candidate should be able to exhibit in the examination;
2 to demonstrate the approach likely to be taken by examiners in examination questions.

The learning outcomes are part of a hierarchy of learning objectives. The verbs used at the beginning of each learning outcome relate to a specific learning objective, e.g. Evaluate alternative approaches to budgeting.

The verb 'evaluate' indicates a high-level learning objective. As learning objectives are hierarchical, it is expected that at this level students will have knowledge of different budgeting systems and methodologies and be able to apply them.

A list of the learning objectives and the verbs that appear in the syllabus learning outcomes and examinations follows.

Learning objectives	*Verbs used*	*Definition*
1 Knowledge		
What you are expected to know	List	Make a list of
	State	Express, fully or clearly, the details of/facts of
	Define	Give the exact meaning of
2 Comprehension		
What you are expected to understand	Describe	Communicate the key features of
	Distinguish	Highlight the differences between
	Explain	Make clear or intelligible/State the meaning of

		Identify	Recognise, establish or select after consideration
		Illustrate	Use an example to describe or explain something
3	Application *How you are expected to apply your knowledge*	Apply	To put to practical use
		Calculate/ compute	To ascertain or reckon mathematically
		Demonstrate	To prove with certainty or to exhibit by practical means
		Prepare	To make or get ready for use
		Reconcile	To make or prove consistent/compatible
		Solve	Find an answer to
		Tabulate	Arrange in a table
4	Analysis *How you are expected to analyse the detail of what you have learned*	Analyse	Examine in detail the structure of
		Categorise	Place into a defined class or division
		Compare and contrast	Show the similarities and/or differences between
		Construct	To build up or compile
		Discuss	To examine in detail by argument
		Interpret	To translate into intelligible or familiar terms
		Produce	To create or bring into existence
5	Evaluation *How you are expected to use your learning to evaluate, make decisions or recommendations*	Advise	To counsel, inform or notify
		Evaluate	To appraise or assess the value of
		Recommend	To advise on a course of action

Computer-based assessment

CIMA has introduced computer-based assessment (CBA) for all subjects at Certificate level.

Objective test questions are used. The most common type is 'multiple choice', where you have to choose the correct answer from a list of possible answers, but there are a variety of other objective questions types that can be used within the system. These include true/false questions, matching pairs of text and graphic, sequencing and ranking, labelling diagrams and single and multiple numeric entry.

Candidates answer the questions by either pointing and clicking the mouse, moving objects around the screen, typing numbers, or a combination of these responses. Try the online demo at [http://www.cimaglobal.com/cba] to get a feel for how the technology works.

The CBA system can ensure that a wide range of the syllabus is assessed, as a pre-determined number of questions from each syllabus area (dependent upon the syllabus weighting for that particular area) are selected in each assessment.

There are two types of questions which were previously involved in objective testing in paper-based exams and which are not at present possible in a CBA. The actual drawing of graphs and charts is not yet possible. Equally there will be no questions calling for comments to be written by students. Charts and interpretations remain on many syllabi and will be examined at Certificate level but using other methods.

For further CBA practice, CIMA Publishing produces CIMA e-success CD-ROMs for all Certificate level subjects. These are available at www.cimapublishing.com.

Fundamentals of Management Accounting and computer-based assessment

The assessment for Fundamentals of Management Accounting is a two hour computer-based assessment comprising 50 compulsory questions, with one or more parts. Single part questions are generally worth 1–2 marks each, but two and three part questions may be worth 4 or 6 marks. There will be no choice and all questions should be attempted if time permits. CIMA are continuously developing the question styles within the CBA system and you are advised to try the on-line website demo at www.cimaglobal.com/cba, to both gain familiarity with assessment software and examine the latest style of questions being used.

Fundamentals of Management Accounting

Syllabus outline

The syllabus comprises:

Topic and study weighting

A	Cost Determination	25%
B	Cost Behaviour and Break-even Analysis	10%
C	Standard Costing	15%
D	Cost and Accounting Systems	30%
E	Financial Planning and Control	20%

Learning aims

This syllabus aims to test student's ability to:

- explain and use concepts and processes to determine product and service costs;
- explain direct, marginal and absorption costs and their use in pricing;
- apply cost–volume–profit (CVP) analysis and interpret the results;
- apply a range of costing and accounting systems;
- explain the role of budgets and standard costing within organisations;
- prepare and interpret budgets, standard costs and variance statements.

Assessment strategy

There will be a computer-based assessment of 2 hours duration, comprising 50 compulsory questions, each with one or more parts.
A variety of objective test question types and styles will be used within the assessment.

Learning outcomes and indicative syllabus content

A Cost Determination – 25%

Learning outcomes

On completion of their studies students should be able to:

- explain why organisations need to know how much products, processes and services cost and why they need costing systems;
- explain the idea of a 'cost object';
- explain the concept of a direct cost and an indirect cost;
- explain why the concept of 'cost' needs to be qualified as direct, full, marginal and so on, in order to be meaningful;
- distinguish between the historical cost of an asset and the economic value of an asset to an organisation;
- apply first-in-first-out (FIFO), last-in-first-out (LIFO) and average cost (AVCO) methods of accounting for inventory, calculating inventory values and related gross profit;
- explain why FIFO is essentially a historical cost method, while LIFO approximates economic cost;
- prepare cost statements for allocation and apportionment of overheads, including between reciprocal service departments;
- calculate direct, variable and full costs of products, services and activities using overhead absorption rates to trace indirect costs to cost units;
- explain the use of cost information in pricing decisions, including marginal cost pricing and the calculation of 'full cost' based prices to generate a specified return on sales or investment.

Indicative syllabus content

- Classification of costs and the treatment of direct costs (specifically attributable to a cost object) and indirect costs (not specifically attributable) in ascertaining the cost of a 'cost object', for example a product, service, activity, customer.
- Cost measurement: historical versus economic costs.
- Accounting for the value of materials on FIFO, LIFO and AVCO bases.
- Overhead costs: allocation, apportionment, re-apportionment and absorption of overhead costs. Note: The repeated distribution method only will be examined for reciprocal service department costs.
- Marginal cost pricing and full cost pricing to achieve specified return on sales or return on investment.

Note: Students are not expected to have a detailed knowledge of activity based costing (ABC).

B Cost Behaviour and Break-even Analysis – 10%

Learning outcomes

On completion of their studies students should be able to:

- explain how costs behave as product, service or activity levels increase or decrease;
- distinguish between fixed, variable and semi-variable costs;
- explain step costs and the importance of time-scales in their treatment as either variable or fixed;

- compute the fixed and variable elements of a semi-variable cost using the high–low method and 'line of best fit' method;
- explain the concept of contribution and its use in cost–volume–profit (CVP) analysis;
- calculate and interpret the break-even point, profit target, margin of safety and profit–volume ratio for a single product or service;
- prepare break-even charts and profit–volume graphs for a single product or service;
- calculate the profit maximising sales mix for a multi-product company that has limited demand for each product and one other constraint or limiting factor.

Indicative syllabus content

- Fixed, variable and semi-variable costs.
- Step costs and the importance of time-scale in analysing cost behaviour.
- High–low and graphical methods to establish fixed and variable elements of a semi-variable cost. Note: regression analysis is not required.
- Contribution concept and CVP analysis.
- Breakeven charts, profit–volume graphs, break-even point, profit target, margin of safety, contribution/sales ratio.
- Limiting factor analysis.

C Standard Costing – 15%

Learning outcomes

On completion of their studies students should be able to:

- explain the difference between ascertaining costs after the event and planning by establishing standard costs in advance;
- explain why planned standard costs, prices and volumes are useful in setting a benchmark for comparison and so allowing managers' attention to be directed to areas of the business that are performing below or above expectation;
- calculate standard costs for the material, labour and variable overhead elements of cost of a product or service;
- calculate variances for materials, labour, variable overhead, sales prices and sales volumes;
- prepare a statement that reconciles budgeted contribution with actual contribution;
- interpret statements of variances for variable costs, sales prices and sales volumes including possible inter-relations between cost variances, sales price and volume variances, and cost and sales variances;
- describe the possible use of standard labour costs in designing incentive schemes for factory and office workers.

Indicative syllabus content

- Principles of standard costing.
- Preparation of standards for the variable elements of cost: material, labour, variable overhead.
- Variances: materials – total, price and usage; labour – total, rate and efficiency; variable overhead – total, expenditure and efficiency; sales – sales price and sales

volume contribution. Note: Students will be expected to calculate the sales volume contribution variance.
- Reconciliation of budgeted and actual contribution.
- Piecework and the principles of incentive schemes based on standard hours versus actual hours taken. Note: The details of a specific incentive scheme will be provided in the examination.

D Costing and Accounting Systems – 30%

Learning outcomes

On completion of their studies students should be able to:

- explain the principles of manufacturing accounts and the integration of the cost accounts with the financial accounting system;
- prepare a set of integrated accounts, given opening balances and appropriate transactional information, and show standard cost variances;
- compare and contrast job, batch, contract and process costing;
- prepare ledger accounts for job, batch and process costing systems;
- prepare ledger accounts for contract costs;
- explain the difference between subjective and objective classifications of expenditure and the importance of tracing costs both to products/services and to responsibility centres;
- construct coding systems that facilitate both subjective and objective classification of costs;
- prepare financial statements that inform management;
- explain why gross revenue, value-added, contribution, gross margin, marketing expense, general and administration expense, and so on might be highlighted in management reporting;
- compare and contrast management reports in a range of organisations including commercial enterprises, charities and public sector undertakings.

Indicative syllabus content

- Manufacturing accounts including raw material, work-in-progress, finished goods and manufacturing overhead control accounts.
- Integrated ledgers including accounting for over- and under-absorption of production overhead.
- The treatment of variances as period entries in integrated ledger systems.
- Job, batch, process and contract costing. Note: Only the average cost method will be examined for process costing but students must be able to deal with differing degrees of completion of opening and closing inventories, normal gains and abnormal gains and losses, and the treatment of scrap value.
- Subjective, objective and responsibility classifications of expenditure and the design of coding systems to facilitate these analyses.
- Cost accounting statements for management information in production and service companies and not-for-profit organisations.

E Financial Planning and Control – 20%

Learning outcomes

On completion of their studies students should be able to:

- explain why organisations set out financial plans in the form of budgets, typically for a financial year;
- prepare functional budgets for material usage and purchase, labour and overheads, including budgets for capital expenditure and depreciation;
- prepare a master budget: income statement, balance sheet and cash flow statement, based on the functional budgets;
- interpret budget statements and advise managers on financing projected cash shortfalls and/or investing projected cash surpluses;
- prepare a flexed budget based on the actual levels of sales and production and calculate appropriate variances;
- compare and contrast fixed and flexed budgets;
- explain the use of budgets in designing reward strategies for managers.

Indicative syllabus content

- Budgeting for planning and control.
- Budget preparation, interpretation and use of the master budget.
- Reporting of actual against budget.
- Fixed and flexible budgeting.
- Budget variances.
- Interpretation and use of budget statements and budget variances.

Examination Techniques

Computer-based examinations

Ten Golden Rules

1. Make sure you are familiar with the software before you start exam. You cannot speak to the invigilator once you have started.
2. These exam practice kits give you plenty of exam style questions to practise.
3. Attempt all questions, there is no negative marking.
4. Double check your answer before you put in the final answer.
5. On multiple choice questions (MCQs), there is only one correct answer.
6. Not all questions will be MCQs – you may have to fill in missing words or figures.
7. Identify the easy questions first and get some points on the board to build up your confidence.
8. Try and allow five minutes at the end to check your answers and make any corrections.
9. If you don't know the answer, try a process of elimination. Sadly there is no phone a friend!
10. Take scrap paper, pen and calculator with you. Work out your answer on paper first if it is easier for you.

1

Cost Behaviour

Cost Behaviour

❓ Concepts and definitions questions

1.1 Distinguish between

    (i) Financial accounting
    (ii) Cost accounting
    (iii) Management accounting

1.2 State six different benefits of cost accounting.

    (i)
    (ii)
    (iii)
    (iv)
    (v)
    (vi)

1.3 Complete the following statements.

    (i) A _____ is a unit of product or service in relation to which costs are ascertained.
    (ii) A _____ cost is an expenditure which can be economically identified with and specifically measured in respect to a relevant cost object.
    (iii) _____ cost is the total cost of direct material, direct labour and direct expenses.
    (iv) An _____ or _____ cost is an expenditure on labour, materials or services which cannot be economically identified with a specific saleable cost unit.
    (v) A cost _____ is a production or service location, function, activity or item of equipment for which costs are accumulated.
    (vi) A _____ cost is a cost which is incurred for an accounting period and which tends to be unaffected by fluctuations in the levels of activity.
    (vii) A _____ cost is a cost which changes in total in relation to the level of output.
    (viii) An example of a fixed cost is _____.
    (ix) An example of a variable cost is _____.
    (x) An example of a semi-fixed/semi-variable cost is _____.

4 Exam Practice Kit: Fundamentals of Management Accounting

1.4 The relationship between total costs Y and activity X is in the form:

$Y = a + bX$

$a =$

$b =$

1.5 Use the high–low method to calculate the fixed and variable elements of the following costs.

	Units	Cost
July	400	£1,000
August	500	£1,200
September	600	£1,400
October	700	£1,600
November	800	£1,800
December	900	£2,000

1.6 Distinguish between

(i) Interpolation
(ii) Extrapolation

1.7 State four limitations of using historical costs to estimate costs to be incurred in the future.

(i)
(ii)
(iii)
(iv)

1.8 The variable production cost per unit of product B is £2 and the fixed production overhead is £4,000. The total production cost of producing 3,000 units of B in a period is £ _____ .

1.9 Describe the scattergraph method of analysing a semi-variable cost into its fixed and variable elements.

1.10 What is a step cost and give an example of one?

✅ Concepts and definitions solutions

1.1 (i) "Financial accounting" is the recording of financial transactions of a firm and a summary of their financial statements within an accounting period for the use of individuals and institutions who wish to analyse and interpret these results.
(ii) "Cost accounting" involves a careful evaluation of the resources used within an organisation. The techniques employed help to provide financial information about the performance of a business and the likely direction which it will take.
(iii) "Management accounting" is essentially concerned with offering advice to management based on financial information gathered and would include budgeting, planning and decision-making.

1.2 Benefits of cost accounting

(i) Discloses profitable and unprofitable parts of the business
(ii) Identifies waste and inefficiency
(iii) Estimates and fixes selling prices
(iv) Values inventories
(v) Develops budgets and standards
(vi) Analyses changes in profits.

1.3 (i) Cost unit
(ii) Direct
(iii) Prime
(iv) Overhead or Indirect
(v) Centre
(vi) Fixed
(vii) Variable
(viii) Rent
(ix) Raw materials
(x) Telephone or Electricity.

1.4 Fixed and variable costs

a = Fixed cost
b = Variable cost

1.5 High–low method

	Units	Cost
Highest month	900	£2,000
Lowest month	400	£1,000
	500	£1,000

The additional cost between the highest and lowest month

$$= \frac{£1,000}{500 \text{ units}} = £2 \text{ per unit}$$

So taking either higher or lower number

Higher 900 × £2 = £1,800   so fixed cost = £200
Lower 400 × £2 = £800   so fixed cost = £200

Under exam conditions choose the number which is easier to calculate.

1.6 Interpolation and Extrapolation

  (i) When a high-low or graphical method has been used to identify the fixed and variable elements of a cost then this may form the basis for cost estimates at different levels of activity.

  (ii) When the level of activity is within the range of activity for which data has been recorded this is known as interpolation.

  (iii) When the level of activity is outside the range of activity for which data has been recorded this is known as extrapolation. This estimate is less likely to be accurate because the assumption that cost behaviour patterns apply outside the recorded range of activities might not be valid.

1.7 Limitations of using historical costs

  (i) Difficult and costly to obtain sufficient data to be sure that a representative sample is used.
  (ii) Implies a continuing relationship of costs to volume.
  (iii) Based on linear relationship between costs and activity.
  (iv) Events in the past may not be representative of the future.

1.8 Total production cost = (3,000 × £2) + £4,000 = £10,000.

1.9 (i) Axes are drawn where the vertical (y) axis is the total cost and the horizontal (x) axis is the level of activity.

  (ii) All recorded data pairs are plotted on the graph as separate points.

  (iii) The straight line of best fit is drawn by eye between the plotted points.

  (iv) The line of best fit is extrapolated back to cross the y axis. The point where the extrapolated line cuts the vertical axis can be read off as the fixed element of the cost.

  (v) The variable element of the cost is established by determining the gradient of the line of best fit.

1.10 Step cost is a cost which rises in a series of steps, for example, the rent of a second factory.

Multiple choice questions

1.1 Which of the following are prime costs?

   (i) Direct materials
   (ii) Direct labour
   (iii) Indirect labour
   (iv) Indirect expenses

   A (i) and (ii)
   B (i) and (iii)
   C (ii) and (iii)
   D (ii) and (iv)

1.2 Which of the following could not be classified as a cost unit?

   A Ream of paper
   B Barrel of beer
   C Chargeable man-hour
   D Hospital

1.3 Which of the following could be a step fixed cost?

   A Direct material cost
   B Electricity cost to operate a packing machine
   C Depreciation cost of the packing machine
   D Depreciation cost of all packing machines in the factory

1.4 Which of the following would be classified as indirect labour?

   A Assembly workers in a car plant
   B Bricklayers in a building company
   C Stores assistants in a factory
   D An auditor in a firm of accountants

1.5 Which of the following would not be classified as a cost centre in a hotel?

   A Restaurant
   B Rooms
   C Bar
   D Meals served

1.6 The information below shows the number of calls made and the monthly telephone bill for the first quarter of the latest year:

Month	No. of calls	Cost
January	400	£1,050
February	600	£1,700
March	900	£2,300

Using the high–low method the costs could be subdivided into:

- A Fixed cost £50   Variable cost per call £2.50
- B Fixed cost £50   Variable cost per call £25
- C Fixed cost £25   Variable cost per call £2.50
- D Fixed cost £25   Variable cost per call £25

1.7 The following data relate to two output levels of a department:

Machine hours	18,000	20,000
Overheads	£380,000	£390,000

The variable overhead rate was £5 per hour.
The amount of fixed overhead was

- A £230,000
- B £240,000
- C £250,000
- D £290,000

1.8 Fixed costs are conventionally deemed to be:

- A Constant per unit of output
- B Constant in total when production volume changes
- C Outside the control of management
- D Those unaffected by inflation

1.9 Which of the following correctly describes a step cost?

- A The total cost increases in steps as the level of inflation increases
- B The cost per unit increases in steps as the level of inflation increases
- C The cost per unit increases in steps as the level of activity increases
- D The total cost increases in steps as the level of activity increases

1.10 Which of the following pairs are the best examples of semi-variable costs?

- A Rent and rates
- B Labour and materials
- C Electricity and gas
- D Road fund licence and petrol

✓ Multiple choice solutions

1.1 A

Prime costs consist of direct materials, direct labour and direct expenses.

1.2 D

Alternatives A, B and C are all examples of cost units. A hospital might be classified as a cost centre.

1.3 D

Cost D could behave in a step fashion over a period of time. The total depreciation cost would remain fixed for a certain number of machines. If an additional machine is required the total cost will increase to a higher level at which it will again remain constant. The addition of further machines will increase the total depreciation cost in successive steps. Cost A is a variable cost, cost B is a semi-variable cost and cost C is a fixed cost.

1.4 C

Alternatives A, B and C are all direct labour. A stores assistant is an example of indirect labour.

1.5 D

This question relates to costs in a hotel. Alternatives A, B and C are all department or cost centres. A meal served would be a cost unit.

1.6 A

	Calls	Cost
Highest	900	£2,300
Lowest	400	£1,050
	500	£1,250

Variable cost = $\dfrac{£1,250}{500}$ = £2.50 per call

Fixed cost = Total cost − variable cost
= £1,050 − (400 × £2.50)
= £1,050 − £1,000
= £50

So fixed cost = £50 and variable cost = £2.50 per call.

1.7 D

The calculation is as follows:
Total cost for 18,000 hours = £380,000
Variable cost = 18,000 × 5 = £90,000
Fixed costs = £290,000

1.8 B

The total amount of fixed costs remains unchanged when production volume changes, therefore the unit rate fluctuates.

1.9 **D**

Cost behaviour patterns refer to the way that the cost behaves in relation to the level of activity. Therefore options A and B are incorrect. Option C describes a non-linear variable cost.

1.10 **C**

The best examples of semi-variable costs are electricity and gas, since there is a cost for the use of the service which is fixed and a further variable cost based on usage.

2

Accounting for
the Value of Inventories

Accounting for the Value of Inventories 2

❓ Concepts and definitions questions

2.1 What is a material requisition?

2.2 What are the three methods of inventory valuation?

   (i)
   (ii)
   (iii)

2.3 In January there was no opening inventory of material and 1,000 tonnes were purchased as follows:

   3rd January   200 tonnes at £50 per tonne
   8th January   400 tonnes at £60 per tonne
   17th January   400 tonnes at £70 per tonne

   During the same period four material requisitions were completed for 200 tonnes each on the 4th, 12th, 18th and 26th of the month. Using the information given, calculate the quantity and value of closing inventory at the end of January using the FIFO method.

2.4 Using the information in Question 2.3, calculate the quantity and value of closing inventory using the LIFO method.

2.5 Using the information in Question 2.3, calculate the value and quantity of closing inventory using the weighted average method.

2.6 What are the advantages and disadvantages of FIFO?

2.7 What are the advantages and disadvantages of LIFO?

2.8 What are the advantages and disadvantages of weighted average pricing?

2.9 What is a perpetual inventory?

2.10 State four advantages of using a material code.

   (i)
   (ii)
   (iii)
   (iv)

14 Exam Practice Kit: Fundamentals of Management Accounting

✓ Concepts and definitions solutions

2.1 A material requisition is used to authorise and record the issue of material from stores to production or for indirect purposes.

2.2 The three methods of inventory valuation are

    (i) FIFO – First In First Out
    (ii) LIFO – Last In First Out
    (iii) Weighted average cost.

2.3 Inventory valuation using FIFO

	Receipts (Issues)			Balance (Quantity)		
Date	Quantity	Price £	Value £	At 50 £	At 60 £	At 70 £
3rd Jan	200	50	10,000	200		
4th Jan	(200)	50	(10,000)	(200)		
8th Jan	400	60	24,000		400	
12th Jan	(200)	60	(12,000)		(200)	
17th Jan	400	70	28,000			400
18th Jan	(200)	60	(12,000)		(200)	
26th Jan	(200)	70	(14,000)			(200)
Closing Balance 31st Jan	200	70	14,000	–	–	200

2.4. Inventory valuation using LIFO

	Receipts (Issues)			Balance (Quantity)		
Date	Quantity	Price £	Value £	At 50 £	At 60 £	At 70 £
3rd Jan	200	50	10,000	200		
4th Jan	(200)	50	(10,000)	(200)		
8th Jan	400	60	24,000		400	
12th Jan	(200)	60	(12,000)		(200)	
17th Jan	400	70	28,000			400
18th Jan	(200)	70	(14,000)			(200)
26th Jan	(200)	70	(14,000)			(200)
Closing Balance 31st Jan	200	60	12,000	–	200	–

Accounting for the Value of Inventories

2.5 Inventory valuation using weighted average

	Receipts (Issues)		
Date	Quantity	Price (£)	Value (£)
3rd Jan	200	50	10,000
4th Jan	(200)	50	(10,000)
8th Jan	400	60	24,000
12th Jan	(200)	60	(12,000)
17th Jan	400	70	28,000
Balance	600	66.66	40,000
18th Jan	(200)	66.66	(13,333)
26th Jan	(200)	66.66	(13,333)
Closing Balance 31st Jan	200	66.66	13,333

2.6 Advantages and disadvantages of FIFO

Advantage

(i) Produces realistic inventory values.

Disadvantages

(i) Produces out-of-date production costs.
(ii) Complicates inventory records since items must be analysed by delivery.

2.7 Advantages and disadvantages of LIFO

Advantage

(i) Produces realistic production cost, therefore more realistic profit figures.

Disadvantages

(i) Produces unrealistic inventory values.
(ii) Complicates inventory records as items must be analysed by delivery.

2.8 Advantages and disadvantages of weighted average price

Advantage

(i) Simple to operate, no need to analyse inventory with every delivery.

Disadvantage

(i) Neither inventory figures nor production costs are realistic.

2.9 Perpetual inventory

Perpetual inventory is the recordings of receipts and issues as they occur showing the balances of individual items of inventory in terms of quantity and value.

2.10 Material coding system

Advantages

(i) Reduces clerical effort
(ii) Avoids ambiguity
(iii) Easier for referral
(iv) Essential when handling mechanical or electronic data.

16 Exam Practice Kit: Fundamentals of Management Accounting

Multiple choice questions

Questions 2.1 and 2.2 are based on the following information:

	Receipts	Issues
Opening balance	200 at £5	7th 400
5th	300 at £4.50	23rd 400
12th	100 at £6	30th 200
22nd	400 at £5.50	
29th	200 at £7	

2.1 If a FIFO system of inventory valuation were used, the value of inventory at the end of the month would be

   A £1,000
   B £1,100
   C £1,200
   D £1,400

2.2 If a LIFO method of stock inventory were used, the material cost of production in the month would be

   A £5,150
   B £5,350
   C £5,450
   D £5,550

2.3 A chemical is bought in a 100-litre container costing £400. Decanting this into one litre bottles results in a 0.5% loss. To cover this loss, each litre bottle would need to be costed at:

   A £3.98
   B £4.00
   C £4.02
   D £4.04

2.4 A system which provides a continuous record of the balance of each inventory item is known as

   A JIT Management
   B An imprest system
   C A perpetual inventory system
   D None of the above

2.5 When goods are delivered by a supplier, the storekeeper will then raise

   A An invoice
   B A customs certificate
   C A goods received note
   D A perpetual inventory system

2.6 The purchase price of Material X is increasing. If the LIFO system of inventory valuation is used, the value of the closing inventory is:

A close to current purchase prices
B higher than current purchase prices
C based on the prices of the latest items received
D based on the prices of the earliest items received

Questions 2.7 to 2.9 are based on the following information:

Opening inventory of product Y is zero. The following receipts and sales occurred during May.

2 May   Received 200 units at a cost of £6.00 each
4 May   Sold 40 units at a price of £14.00 each
15 May   Received 40 units at a cost of £7.25 each
22 May   Sold 60 units at a price of £14.50 each

2.7 If the perpetual weighted average method is used to value inventory, the value of the closing inventory will be:

A £869.17
B £875.00
C £927.50
D £1,995.00

2.8 If a FIFO inventory valuation method is used, the value of the closing inventory will be:

A £600
B £840
C £890
D £1,015

2.9 If a LIFO inventory valuation method is used, the gross profit for the period will be:

A £780
B £800
C £830
D £840

2.10 Which of the following documents is used to record the issue of materials from stores to a production cost centre?

A Goods received note
B Material requisition
C Materials transfer note
D Materials returned note

18 Exam Practice Kit: Fundamentals of Management Accounting

✓ Multiple choice solutions

2.1 **D**

Receipts = 1,200
Issues = 1,000
Closing inventory (200 × £7) = £1,400

2.2 **C**

	£
Total value of receipts	6,550
Less: Closing inventory	

	£	
100 × £5	500	
100 × £6	600	
		1,100
		5,450

2.3 **C**

Each bottle needs to be issued at $\dfrac{400}{99.5}$ = £4.02

2.4 **C**

2.5 **C**

2.6 **D**

LIFO prices issues at the price of the latest items received. Therefore the remaining inventory is valued at the oldest prices.

2.7 **B**

	Receipts				Sales				Balance	
Qty	Cost	£	Qty	Cost	£	Qty	Cost	£
200	6.00	1,200				200	6.00	1,200
			40	6.00	240	160	6.00	960
40	7.25	290				160	6.00	960
						40	7.25	290
						200	6.25	1,250
			60	6.25	375	140	6.25	875

2.8 C

	Receipts			Sales			Balance	
Qty	Cost	£	Qty	Cost	£	Qty	Cost	£
200	6.00	1,200				200	6.00	1,200
			40	6.00	240	160	6.00	960
40	7.25	290				160	6.00	960
						40	7.25	290
						200		1,250
			60	6.00	360	100	6.00	600
						40	7.25	290
						140		890

2.9 A

	Receipts			Sales			Balance	
Qty	Cost	£	Qty	Cost	£	Qty	Cost	£
200	6.00	1,200				200	6.00	1,200
			40	6.00	240	160	6.00	960
40	7.25	290				160	6.00	960
						40	7.25	290
						200		1,250
			40	7.25	290			
			20	6.00	120			
			60		410	140	6.00	840

Gross profit = (40 × £14) + (60 × £14.50) − £(240 + 410) = £780

2.10 B

A material requisition is used to ensure that the correct cost centre is charged with the cost of the material.

3

Overhead Costs: Allocation, Apportionment and Absorption

Overhead Costs: Allocation, Apportionment and Absorption 3

? Concepts and definitions questions

3.1 What are the three main ways in which indirect production costs are incurred?

  (i)
  (ii)
  (iii)

3.2 To attribute overhead costs to cost units, what are the five steps which must be taken?

  (i) *Step 1*
  (ii) *Step 2*
  (iii) *Step 3*
  (iv) *Step 4*
  (v) *Step 5*

3.3 By what basis would you apportion the following cost?

  (i) Rent
  (ii) Power
  (iii) Depreciation
  (iv) Cost of canteen facility
  (v) Machine maintenance labour
  (vi) Supervision

3.4 A company occupies 100,000 sq. metres with an annual rent of £500,000. Department A takes up 30,000 sq. metres, Department B uses 20,000 sq. metres and Department C and D use 25,000 sq. metres each. How much rent should be apportioned to Department A?

24 Exam Practice Kit: Fundamentals of Management Accounting

3.5 A company has three production departments A, B and C and two service departments X and Y.

Overheads have been attributed to these departments as follows:

Department	£
A	100,000
B	75,000
C	50,000
X	25,000
Y	10,000

An analysis of the services provided by each service department shows the following percentages of total time spent for the benefit of each department.

Service department	Production			Service department	
	A	B	C	X	Y
X	30	30	20	–	20
Y	50	10	30	10	–

Calculate the costs attributed to production departments A, B and C.

3.6 State five methods by which overheads can be absorbed into cost units.

(i)
(ii)
(iii)
(iv)
(v)

Questions 3.7–3.10 are based on the following information:

A manufacturing company uses pre-determined rates for absorbing overheads based on the budgeted level of activity. A rate of £22 per labour hour has been calculated for the Assembly Department for which the following overhead expenditures at various activity levels have been estimated.

Assembly department total overheads £	Number of labour hours
338,875	14,500
347,625	15,500
356,375	16,500

3.7 Calculate (i) the variable overhead absorption rate per labour hour and (ii) the estimated total fixed overheads.

3.8 Calculate the budgeted level of activity in labour hours.

3.9 Calculate the amount of under/over absorption of overheads, if the actual labour hours were 15,850 and actual overheads were £355,050.

3.10 What are the arguments both for and against using departmental absorption rates as opposed to a single factory-wide rate?

Overhead Costs: Allocation, Apportionment and Absorption **25**

✓ Concepts and definitions solutions

3.1 The three main ways in which indirect production costs incurred are

  (i) Production activities, for example, supervision
  (ii) Service activities, for example, stores
  (iii) Establishment costs, for example, heating and lighting.

3.2 Five steps taken to attribute overhead costs to cost units are

Step 1 – Collect production overhead by item
Step 2 – Establish cost centres
Step 3 – Allocate and apportion overhead costs to cost centres
Step 4 – Apportion service cost centre costs to production cost centres
Step 5 – Absorb production cost centre costs into cost units.

3.3 Cost apportionment

  (i) Rent – Floor space
  (ii) Power – Kilowatt hours
  (iii) Depreciation – Capital value
  (iv) Cost of canteen facility – No. of workers
  (v) Machine maintenance labour – Machine maintenance hours
  (vi) Supervision – No. of workers.

3.4 Rent apportionment

Total occupancy	= 100,000 sq. metres
Annual rent	= £500,000
Cost per sq. metre	= £5
Department A occupancy	= 30,000 sq. metres
Department A rent (30,000 × £5)	= £150,000

3.5 Production and services department

	Production (£)			Service (£)	
	A	B	C	X	Y
Initial Allocation	100,000	75,000	50,000	25,000	10,000
Apportion X	7,500	7,500	5,000	(25,000)	5,000
Apportion Y	7,500	1,500	4,500	1,500	(15,000)
Apportion X	450	450	300	(1,500)	300
Apportion Y	150	30	90	30	(300)
Apportion X	11	11	8	*(30)	–
Total charge for overhead	115,611	84,491	59,898	–	–

  * When the service department cost reduces to a small amount, the final apportionment is adjusted for roundings.

3.6 Methods by which overheads can be absorbed into cost units

    (i)   Rate per unit
    (ii) Percentage of prime cost
    (iii) Percentage of direct wages
    (iv) Direct labour hour rate
    (v) Machine hour rate.

3.7 Variable and fixed overheads

    (i)   Variable overhead absorption rate using high–low method

$$\frac{£356,375 - £338,875}{16,500 - 14,500} = £8.75 \text{ per hour}$$

    (ii) At 14,500 labour hours

	£
Total overheads expected	338,875
Variable overheads (14,500 × £8.75)	(126,875)
Estimated total fixed overheads	212,000

3.8 Budgeted level of labour hours

Total budgeted overheads = £22 per hour

Variable overheads = £8.75 per hour

Therefore fixed overheads = £13.25 per hour

$$\frac{£212,000}{£13.25} = 16,000 \text{ labour hours.}$$

3.9 *Under/over absorption*

	£
Actual overheads	355,050
Absorbed overheads (15,850 × £22)	(348,700)
Under absorption of overheads	6,350

3.10 Arguments for and against departmental absorption rates:

For

    (i)   Costings of products are more accurate since each product can be charged with the relevant amount of overheads from each department.
    (ii) Cost control is improved since under/over absorption can be calculated for each department.

Against

    (i)   A single factory-wide rate is simpler, less time-consuming and cheaper.
    (ii) If departmental rates are not kept under constant review, they may give misleading costing information.

Overhead Costs: Allocation, Apportionment and Absorption

Multiple choice questions

3.1 What are the three objectives of accounting for overhead costs?

  (i) To identify costs in relation to output products or services
  (ii) To identify costs in relation to activities and divisions of the organisation
  (iii) To identify and control overhead costs
  (iv) To identify and control direct costs

  A (i) and (ii)
  B (i), (ii) and (iii)
  C (i), (ii) and (iv)
  D (i), (ii), (iii) and (iv)

3.2 There are three departments in a factory.

Department A occupies 2,000 sq. metres
Department B occupies 2,500 sq. metres
Department C occupies 500 sq. metres
Annual rent = £40,000

The combined rent apportioned to Department A and B is

  A £16,000
  B £20,000
  C £24,000
  D £36,000

3.3 A company has four production departments. Fixed overhead costs are as follows:

Department	£	Hours taken
A	10,000	5
B	5,000	5
C	4,000	4
D	6,000	3

The company produces one product and the time spent in each department is shown above. If overhead is recovered on the basis of labour hours and budgeted production is 2,000 units, the fixed overhead cost per unit is

  A £3
  B £12
  C £12.50
  D £17.50

3.4 Budgeted overhead   = £100,000
    Actual overhead   = £90,000
    Budgeted labour hours   = 20,000
    Actual labour hours   = 21,000

Calculate the amount of under/over absorption of overheads.

  A Over absorption £15,000
  B Over absorption £5,000
  C Under absorption £15,000
  D Under absorption £5,000

3.5 A method of accounting for overheads involves attributing them to cost units using predetermined rates. This is known as

A overhead allocation
B overhead apportionment
C overhead absorption
D overhead analysis

3.6 A company absorbs overheads on standard machine hours which were budgeted at 11,250 with overheads of £258,750. Actual results were 10,980 standard machine hours with overheads of £254,692.
Overheads were:

A under-absorbed by £2,152
B over-absorbed by £4,058
C under-absorbed by £4,058
D over-absorbed by £2,152

The following data relate to questions 3.7 and 3.8

Budgeted machine hours	22,000
Actual machine hours	23,500
Budgeted production overhead	£99,000
Actual production overhead	£111,625

3.7 The machine hour rate for overhead absorption is

A £0.22
B £4.22
C £4.50
D £4.75

3.8 The amount of under/over absorption is

A £5,875 under-absorbed
B £5,875 over-absorbed
C £12,625 under-absorbed
D £12,625 over-absorbed

3.9 A method of dealing with overheads involves spreading common costs over cost centres on the basis of benefit received. This is known as

A Overhead absorption
B Overhead apportionment
C Overhead allocation
D Overhead analysis

3.10 A vehicle repair company recovers overhead on the basis of chargeable labour hours. Budgeted overheads for the latest period were £28,800 and actual chargeable labour hours worked were 400. The actual overheads of £26,700 were over-absorbed by £2,280.
The budgeted overhead absorption rate per chargeable labour hour was:

A £61.05
B £66.75
C £72.00
D £72.45

Overhead Costs: Allocation, Apportionment and Absorption

✓ Multiple choice solutions

3.1 B

Alternatives (i), (ii) and (iii) are all concerned with overheads. Direct costs are prime costs.

3.2 D

$$\text{Rent Department A} = \frac{2,000}{5,000} \times £40,000 = £16,000$$

$$\text{Rent Department B} = \frac{2,500}{5,000} \times £40,000 = £20,000$$

So Department A + Department B = £16,000 + £20,000
= £36,000

3.3 C

Total fixed overhead cost = £10,000 + £5,000 + £4,000 + £6,000
= £25,000
Budgeted production = 2,000 units
Fixed overhead cost per unit = $\frac{£25,000}{2,000}$
= £12.50

3.4 A

Budgeted overhead rate per hour

$$= \frac{\text{Budgeted overhead}}{\text{Budgeted hours}} = \frac{£100,000}{20,000} = £5$$

Actual hours × standard rate (21,000 × £5) = £105,000
Actual overhead = £90,000
Over absorption = £15,000

3.5 C

Overhead allocation is the allotment of whole items of cost to cost units or cost centres. Overhead apportionment is the sharing out of costs over a number of cost centres according to the benefit used. Overhead analysis refers to the whole process of recording and accounting for overheads.

3.6 A

$$\text{Overhead absorption rate} = \frac{£258,750}{11,250} = £23 \text{ per standard machine hour}$$

	£
Overhead absorbed = 10,980 std. hours × £23	252,540
Overhead incurred	254,692
Under absorption	2,152

3.7 **C**

Machine hour rate = £99,000/22,000 = £4.50 per machine hour

3.8 **A**

	£
Overhead absorbed (23,500 hours × £4.50)	105,750
Overhead incurred	111,625
Under-absorbed overhead	(5,875)

3.9 **B**

A method of dealing with overheads which involves spreading common costs over cost centres on the basis of benefit received is known as overhead apportionment.

3.10 **D**

	£
Actual overheads incurred	26,700
Over absorption	2,280
Overhead absorbed by actual hours	28,980
Overhead rate per hour = £28,980/400	£72.45

4

Cost–Volume–Profit Analysis

Cost–Volume–Profit Analysis 4

❓ Concepts and definitions questions

4.1 What is contribution?

4.2 What is a limiting factor?

4.3 Break-even analysis

Consider the following data:

Selling price   £10 per unit
Variable cost   £6 per unit
Fixed costs   £1,000

How many units need to be sold to break even?

4.4 Profit targets

Using the same data as in Question 4.3, if fixed costs rise by 20% and the company need to make a profit of £350, how many units need to be sold?

4.5 Margin of safety

If budgeted production and sales are 80,000 units and selling price is £10, variable cost is £5 per unit and fixed costs are £200,000, calculate the margin of safety.

4.6 A product has an operating statement for the sales of 1,000 units.

	£
Sales	10,000
Variable costs	6,000
Fixed costs	2,500

You are required to calculate:

(i) Profitability to sales
(ii) Contribution to sales

(iii) Break-even sales in
(1) value
(2) units
(iv) Margin of safety

4.7 State four assumptions of CVP analysis.

(i)
(ii)
(iii)
(iv)

4.8 What is the difference between a break-even chart and a profit-volume chart?

4.9 Why does an economist's break-even chart differ from that of an accountant?

4.10 A company makes two products which both use the same type and grade of materials and labour but in different quantities.

	Product A	Product B
Labour hours	5	8
Materials/unit	£20	£15

During each week there are 2,000 labour hours available and the value of material available is limited to £12,000.

Product A makes a contribution of £5 per unit and product B earns £6 contribution per unit.

Which product should they make?

4.11 A company makes three products X, Y and Z. All three products use the same type of labour which is limited to 1,000 hours per month. Individual details are as follows:

Product	X	Y	Z
Contribution/unit	£25	£40	£32
Labour hours/unit	5	6	8
Maximum demand	50	100	400

What quantities of each product should they produce?

✅ Concepts and definitions solutions

4.1 Contribution = sales value minus variable cost.

4.2 A limiting factor is any factor which is in scarce supply and stops the organisation from expanding its activities further.

In such a situation, it then seeks to maximise the contribution per unit of the limiting factor.

4.3 Break-even volume target

$$\text{Break-even volume target} = \frac{\text{Fixed costs}}{\text{Selling price} - \text{variable cost per unit}}$$

$$= \frac{£1,000}{£10 - £6} = 250 \text{ units}$$

4.4 Profit targets

$$\text{Volume target} = \frac{\text{Contribution target}}{\text{Unit contribution}}$$

$$= \frac{£1,000 + £200 + £350}{£4} = 387.5$$

So rounding up 388 units.

4.5 Margin of safety

The margin of safety is the difference between budgeted sales volume and break-even sales volume.

$$\text{Break-even sales} = \frac{£200,000}{£10 - £5} = 40,000 \text{ units}$$

Budgeted sales = 80,000

So margin of safety = 40,000 or 50% of budgeted sales.

4.6 (i) Profitability to sales $= \dfrac{£1,500}{£10,000} = 15\%$

(ii) Contribution to sales $= \dfrac{£4,000}{£10,000} = 40\%$

(iii) 1 Break-even sales value $= \dfrac{£2,500}{40\%} = £6,250$

2 If selling price is £10 and break-even sales value is £6,250 then unit sales = 625

(iv) Margin of safety $= \dfrac{£3,750 \; (£10,000 - £6,250)}{£10,000}$

$$= 37.5\%$$

If you multiply contribution to sales ratio with margin of safety, you end up with the same figure as the profitability to sales ratio.

36 Exam Practice Kit: Fundamentals of Management Accounting

4.7 Assumption of CVP analysis

　(i)　Assumes selling price is constant, regardless of the number of units sold.
　(ii)　Assumes fixed costs are constant.
　(iii)　Assumes variable cost per unit is constant.
　(iv)　Assumes that activity level is the only factor affecting cost.

4.8 Break-even chart vs profit-volume chart

A break-even chart plots total costs and total revenues at different levels of output.

A profit-volume chart shows the net profit or loss at any level of output.

4.9 For the accountant, both the total cost and sales revenue are shown as straight lines. For the economist, unit cost could rise or fall due to economies or diseconomies of scale and in order to sell more units, the economist would argue that price would need to fall.

4.10 Multiple products

Labour hours (2,000/5) = 400 units of A
Labour hours (2,000/8) = 250 units of B
Materials (£12,000/£20) = 600 units of A
Materials (£12,000/£15) = 800 units of B

Limiting factor is labour.

So

Product A contribution per labour hour $= \dfrac{£5}{5} = £1$

Product B contribution per labour hour $= \dfrac{£6}{8} = £0.75$

Company maximises its contribution by selling product A, since limiting factor value is higher.

4.11 Contribution per labour hour of X $= \dfrac{£25}{5} = £5$　(2nd)

Contribution per labour hour of Y $= \dfrac{£40}{6} = £6.67$　(1st)

Contribution per labour hour of Z $= \dfrac{£32}{8} = £4$　(3rd)

Quantities produced

	Hours
100 units of Y	600
50 units of X	250
18.75 units of Z	150 (balance)
	1,000

Since it would not be practical to produce 0.75 of a unit, we would produce 18 units of product Z with 6 spare hours.

Multiple choice questions

Questions 4.1–4.3 are based on the following information:

A company manufactures a single product which has the following cost structure based on a production and sales budget of 10,000 units.

	£
Direct materials (4 kg at £3 per kg)	12
Direct labour hours (5 hours at £7 per hour)	35

Variable overheads are incurred at £8 per direct labour hour.

Other costs include

	£
Fixed production overheads	120,000
Selling and distribution overheads	160,000
Fixed administration overheads	80,000

The selling and distribution overheads include a variable element due to a distribution cost of £2 per unit. Selling price is £129 per unit.

4.1 How many units must be sold for the company to break even?

  A 8,500
  B 9,000
  C 9,500
  D 1,000

4.2 The level of revenue which would give a net profit of £40,000 is

  A £1,000,000
  B £1,225,500
  C £1,300,250
  D £1,325,000

4.3 The margin of safety is

  A 1,000 units
  B 1,250 units
  C 1,440 units
  D 1,500 units

4.4 If both the selling price and the variable cost per unit of a product rise by 20%, the break-even point will

  A Remain constant
  B Increase
  C Decrease
  D Impossible to determine

4.5 For the forthcoming year, variable costs are budgeted to be 60% of sales value and fixed costs to be 10% of sales value. If the selling price increases by 10% and fixed

38 Exam Practice Kit: Fundamentals of Management Accounting

costs, variable costs per unit and sales volume remain the same, the effect on contribution would be

A A decrease of 5%
B No change
C An increase of 15%
D An increase of 25%

4.6 The selling price is £100, gross profit is 50%. Which one of the following statements is true?

A Mark up is 50%
B Mark up is 100%
C Mark up is 150%
D Mark up is impossible to determine without knowing unit cost.

4.7 Product X generates a contribution to sales ratio of 50%. Fixed costs directly attributable to product X are £100,000 per annum.

The sales revenue required to achieve an annual profit of £125,000 is

A £450,000
B £400,000
C £125,000
D £100,000

4.8 In order to draw a basic break-even chart, which of the following information would you not require?

A Selling price
B Variable cost per unit
C Fixed cost
D Margin of safety

4.9 A company makes a single product which it sells for £10 per unit. Fixed costs are £48,000 and contribution to sales is 40%. If sales were £140,000, what was the margin of safety in units?

A 2,000
B 3,000
C 4,000
D 5,000

4.10 JB produces three products A, B and C which all require skilled labour. This is limited to 6,100 hours per month.

	A	B	C
Labour hours per unit	1	3	1.5
Contribution per unit	£30	£45	£30
Maximum sales	2,500 units	1,000 units	2,000 units

In order to maximise profits for the month, production quantities of each product should be

A A 2,500   B 200   C 2,000
B A 2,500   B 1,000 C 2,000

C A 2,500 B 1,000 C 1,000
D A 2,000 B 1,000 C 2,000

4.11 Company blue makes a single product which requires £5 of materials, 2 hours of labour and 1 hour of machine time.

There is £500 available for materials each week, 80 hours of labour and 148 hours of machine time. The limiting factor is

A Materials
B Labour
C Machine time
D All of the above

4.12 A company makes three products as follows:

	A £	B £	C £
Material at £5 per kg	5	2.50	10
Labour at £2 per hour	6	2	2
Fixed costs absorbed	6	2	2
Profit	6	3.50	5
Selling price	23	10	19

Maximum demand is 1,000 each, materials are limited to 4,000 kg, labour is fixed at 1,000 hours. To maximise profits the company should produce

A 1,000 of A
B 1,000 of B
C 1,000 of C
D 333 of each product

40 Exam Practice Kit: Fundamentals of Management Accounting

✅ Multiple choice solutions

4.1 **A**

Total variable cost	£
Materials (4 kg at £3 per kg)	12
Direct labour hours (5 hours at £7 per hour)	35
Variable overheads (5 hours at £8 per hour)	40
Distribution	2
	89

	£
Selling price	129
Variable cost	89
Contribution per unit	40

Fixed costs	£
Fixed overheads	120,000
Selling and distribution	140,000
Administration	80,000
	340,000

$$= \frac{£340,000}{£40} = 8,500 \text{ units.}$$

4.2 **B**

	£
Total fixed costs	340,000
Profits required	40,000
Required contribution	380,000

$$= \frac{£380,000}{£40} = 9,500 \text{ units}$$

Revenue = 9,500 × £129 = £1,225,500.

4.3 **D**

	Units
Budgeted production and sales	10,000
Break-even sales	8,500
Margin of safety	1,500

4.4 **C**

Assuming selling price is above variable cost, contribution per unit will rise so fewer units need to be sold so break-even will fall.

4.5 D

Let us take a numerical example:

	Original	Change	New
Selling price	100	+10%	110
Variable cost	60	–	60
Contribution/unit	40	+10	50

Percentage increase in contribution per unit = 10/40
= 25% increase.

4.6 B

If gross profit is 50%, unit cost is 50% of the sales price. If unit cost is £50 and selling price is £100, then it has been marked up by a factor of 100%.

4.7 A

$$\frac{\text{Required contribution}}{\text{C/S ratio}} = \frac{£100{,}000 + £125{,}000}{0.5} = £450{,}000$$

4.8 D

The margin of safety can be determined once the chart has been constructed. It is not necessary to know the margin of safety in order to draw the chart.

4.9 A

$$\text{Break-even point} = \frac{\text{Fixed costs}}{\text{Contribution/sales}} = \frac{£48{,}000}{0.4} = £120{,}000$$

If actual sales = £140,000

Margin of safety = £140,000 − £120,000
= £20,000

If selling price = £10 then 2,000 units represents margin of safety.

4.10 A

Limiting factor labour hours

Contribution per limiting factor

	A	B	C
	£30	£15	£20
Rank	1	3	2

	Units	Hours
Product A	2,500	2,500
Product C	2,000	3,000
Product B	200	600
		6,100

4.11 B

Resources available

Materials   = £500
Labour hours = 80
Machine hours = 148

Units we could make from materials	100
Labour	40
Machine time	148

Therefore, limiting factor is labour.

4.12 C

To make 1,000 units of each requires 3,500 kg of material and 5,000 labour hours. Labour is therefore the limiting factor.

To measure contribution we need to add fixed costs absorbed to the profit, so

$$A = \frac{£12}{3} = £4$$

$$B = \frac{£5.50}{1} = £5.50$$

$$C = \frac{£7}{1} = £7$$

Therefore to maximise profits, the company should produce 1,000 units of C.

5

Standard Costs

Standard Costs 5

? Concepts and definitions questions

5.1 What is standard costing?

5.2 What is a standard cost?

5.3 Distinguish between four types of standard.

(i)
(ii)
(iii)
(iv)

5.4 Write down the four cost elements for a standard cost.

(i)
(ii)
(iii)
(iv)

5.5 What is a standard hour?

5.6 A factory had an activity level of 110% with the following output.

	Units	Standard minutes each
Product A	5,000	5
Product B	2,500	10
Product C	3,000	15

The budgeted direct labour cost was £5,000

Calculate:

(i) The budgeted standard hours
(ii) Budgeted labour cost per standard hour

5.7 Annie's cafe makes sandwiches for sale. Contents of their cheese and pickle sandwich are as follows:

2 slices of bread
50 grams of cheese
25 grams of pickle
5 grams of butter

Losses due to accidental damage are estimated to be 5% of the materials input.

Materials can be bought from the cash and carry at the following prices:

Bread 50p per loaf of 20 slices
Cheese £3 per kg
Pickle £2 per kg
Butter £1.50 per kg

Prepare the standard cost of one cheese and pickle sandwich.

5.8 Give five possible sources of information from which a standard materials price may be estimated.

(i)
(ii)
(iii)
(iv)
(v)

5.9 Standard raw materials consist of
  5 kg A at £2 per kg
  3 kg B at £3 per kg

Standard labour consists of
  4 hours grade X at £5 per hour
  5 hours grade Y at £10 per hour

Standard variable overheads are
  9 hours at £20 per hour

Prepare a standard cost card extract to show the standard variable cost.

5.10 In setting standards, three things should be kept in mind. They are

(i)
(ii)
(iii)

Standard Costs **47**

✓ Concepts and definitions solutions

5.1 Standard costing is a control technique which compares standard costs and revenues with actual results to obtain variances which are used to improve performance.

5.2 A standard cost is the planned unit cost of the products, components or services produced in a period.

5.3 Types of standard

(i) A *basic standard* is a standard established for use over a long period from which a current standard can be developed.
(ii) An *ideal standard* is one which can be attained under the most favourable conditions, with no allowance for normal losses, waste or idle time.
(iii) An *attainable standard* is one which can be attained if a standard unit of work is carried out efficiently. Allowances are made for normal losses.
(iv) A *current standard* is based on current levels of performance. Allowances are made for current levels of loss and idle time, etc.

5.4 Preparations of standard costs

In general, a standard cost will be subdivided into four key cost elements. They are

(i) Direct materials
(ii) Direct wages
(iii) Variable overhead
(iv) Fixed overhead.

5.5 A standard hour is the amount of work achievable, at standard efficiency levels in an hour.

5.6 (i) Budgeted labour costs and standard hours

Actual standard hours produced

Product A $\left(5{,}000 \times \dfrac{5}{60}\right)$ 416.67

Product B $\left(2{,}500 \times \dfrac{10}{60}\right)$ 416.67

Product C $\left(3{,}000 \times \dfrac{15}{60}\right)$ 750.00

    1,583.34

Representing 110% of budgeted standard hours

= $1{,}583.34 \times \dfrac{100}{110}$

= 1,439 budgeted standard hours

(ii) Budgeted labour cost per standard hour

$$= \frac{\text{Budgeted cost}}{\text{Budgeted standard hours}}$$

$$= \frac{£5{,}000}{1{,}439}$$

$$= £3.47 \text{ per hour}$$

5.7 Standard cost for cheese and pickle sandwich

	£
2 slices of bread (2 × 2.5p)	0.05
50 grams cheese (5% × £3)	0.15
25 grams pickle (2½% × £2)	0.05
5 grams butter (0.05 × £1.50)	0.0075
Cost per sandwich started 95%	0.2575p
Standard material cost	0.2710p

5.8 Sources of information

Standard materials price may be estimated from:

(i) Quotes/estimates from suppliers
(ii) Industry trends
(iii) Bulk discounts available
(iv) Quality of material
(v) Packaging and carriage inwards charges.

5.9

	£
5 kgs A at £2	10
3 kgs B at £3	9
4 hours grade X at £5	20
5 hours grade Y at £10	50
Variable overhead (9 × £20)	180
Standard variable cost	269

5.10 Standards

In setting standards, three things should be remembered.

(i) Their use for control purposes
(ii) Their impact on motivation
(iii) Their relevance to the planning process.

Multiple choice questions

5.1 Standards which can be attained under the most favourable conditions, with no allowance for idle time or losses are known as:

    A Basic
    B Ideal
    C Attainable
    D Current

5.2 A standard established for use over a long period of time from which a current standard can be developed is a:

    A Basic
    B Ideal
    C Attainable
    D Current

Questions 5.3 and 5.4 are based on the following information:

In a given week, a factory has an activity level of 120% with the following output:

	Units	Standard minutes each
Product A	5,100	6
Product B	2,520	10
Product C	3,150	12

The budgeted direct labour cost for budgeted output was £2,080.

5.3 Budgeted standard hours were

    A 1,560
    B 1,872
    C 1,248
    D 1,300

5.4 Budgeted labour cost per standard hour was

    A £1.33
    B £1.11
    C £1.67
    D £1.60

5.5 A standard hour is

    A Always equivalent to a clock hour
    B An hour with no idle time
    C The quantity of work achievable at standard performance in an hour
    D An hour through which the same products are made

5.6 Which of the following statements is incorrect?

    A Both budgets and standards relate to the future
    B Both budgets and standards must be quantified
    C Both budgets and standards are used in planning
    D Both budgets and standards are expressed in unit costs

5.7 Which type of standard would be most suitable from a motivational point of view?

A Basic
B Ideal
C Attainable
D Current

5.8 Which of the following are criticisms of standard costing?

(i) Standard costing was developed when the business environment was stable
(ii) Performance to standard used to be deemed to be satisfactory but today companies are seeking constant improvement
(iii) Emphasis on labour variances is no longer appropriate with the increasing use of automated production techniques

A (i) and (ii)
B (i) and (iii)
C (ii) and (iii)
D (i), (ii) and (iii)

Questions 5.9 and 5.10 are based on the following data:

Extracts from Company A's records for July –

The standard cost for a single product during July shows the standard direct material content to be 4 litres at £3 per litre.

Actual results were as follows:

Production   1,250
Materials used   5,100 litres @ £15,500

All materials were purchased and used during the same period.

5.9 The material price variance for the period was:

A £500F
B £500A
C £200F
D £200A

5.10 The material usage for the period was:

A £500F
B £500A
C £200F
D £200A

✅ Multiple choice solutions

5.1 B

Standards which can be attained under the most favourable conditions, with no allowance for idle time or losses are known as ideal standards.

5.2 A

A standard established for use over a long period of time from which a current standard can be developed is a basic standard.

5.3 D

Actual standard hours produced

	Hours
Product A $\left(5{,}100 \times \dfrac{6}{60}\right)$	510
Product B $\left(2{,}520 \times \dfrac{10}{60}\right)$	420
Product C $\left(3{,}150 \times \dfrac{12}{60}\right)$	630
	1,560

Budget standard hours $= 1{,}560 \times \dfrac{100}{120} = 1{,}300$

5.4 D

Budgeted labour cost per standard hour

$= \dfrac{\text{Budgeted cost}}{\text{Budgeted standard hours}}$

$= \dfrac{£2{,}080}{1{,}300} = £1.60$

5.5 C

A standard hour is the quantity of work achievable at standard performance in an hour.

5.6 D

Standards are expressed in unit costs. Budgets are expressed in aggregate terms.

5.7 C

An attainable standard is achievable if work is carried out efficiently. An ideal standard can have a negative motivational impact because it makes no allowances for unavoidable losses or idle time, etc. A basic standard is out of date and unrealistic as a basis for monitoring performance. A current standard is based on current levels of performance and so does not provide any incentive for extra effort.

5.8 **D**

5.9 **B**

The material price variance for the period was:

5,000 litres did cost	£15,500
5,000 litres should have cost	£15,000
	£500A

5.10 **D**

The material usage for the period was:

5,100 litres did cost	£15,500
5,100 litres should have cost	£15,300
	£200A

6

Variance Analysis

Variance Analysis 6

❓ Concepts and definitions questions

6.1 What is a cost variance?

6.2 What would an adverse materials price variance and a favourable materials usage variance indicate and what might this be caused by?

6.3 What does an adverse variable overhead efficiency variance indicate and what might be the cause?

6.4 What is the relationship between the labour efficiency variance and the variable overhead efficiency variance? Why might the monetary value be different?

6.5 Sales variances

Budgeted sales	500 units
Actual sales	480 units
Budgeted selling price	£100
Actual selling price	£110
Variable cost per unit	£50
Fixed cost per unit	£15

Calculate

(i) Sales price variance
(ii) Sales volume variance using absorption costing
(iii) Sales volume variance using marginal costing

6.6 Labour variances

Actual production	700 units
Standard wage	£4 per hour
Standard time allowed per unit	1.5 hours
Actual hours worked	1,000 hours
Actual wages paid	£4200

Calculate

(i) Labour rate variance
(ii) Labour efficiency variance

6.7 Fixed overhead variances

Budgeted cost	£44,000
Budgeted production	8,000 units
Budgeted labour hours	16,000 hours
Actual cost	£47,500
Actual production	8450 units
Actual labour hours	16,600 hours

Calculate

(i) Fixed overhead expenditure variance
(ii) Fixed overhead volume variance
(iii) Fixed overhead capacity variance
(iiii) Fixed overhead efficiency variance

6.8 Materials variances

Standard cost 2kg at	£10 per kg
Actual output	1,000 units
Materials purchased and used	2250 kg
Material cost	£20,500

Calculate material price and usage variances

6.9 Explain briefly the possible causes of

(i) The material usage variance;
(ii) The labour rate variance;
(iii) The sales volume contribution variance.

6.10 Explain the meaning and relevance of interdependence of variances when reporting to managers.

✅ Concepts and definitions solutions

6.1 A cost variance is a difference between a planned, budgeted or standard cost and the actual cost incurred.

6.2 Materials variances

An adverse materials price variance and a favourable materials usage variance indicates that there is an inverse relationship between the two. This might be caused by purchasing higher quality material.

6.3 Variable overhead

It indicates that the work completed took longer than it should have done. It could be caused by employing semi-skilled workers instead of skilled workers who will take longer to complete the job.

6.4 Labour/overhead efficiency variance

The labour efficiency variance and the variable overhead efficiency variance will total the same number of hours. Their monetary value is likely to be different if their hourly rates are different.

6.5

    (i) 480 × £110 − £100 = £4800 F
    (ii) 20 × 35 = £700 A
    (iii) 20 × 50 = £1,000 A

6.6

(i)	1,000 hours should cost	£4,000
	1,000 hours did cost	£4200
	So direct labour rate	£200 A
(ii)	700 units should take	1050 hours
	700 units did take	1,000 hours
	A saving of	50 hours
	So 50 × £4 =	£200 F

6.7

(i)	Expenditure variance	
	Should have cost	£44,000
	Did cost	£47500
	So £3500 higher	£3500 A
(ii)	Volume variance	
	Budget	16,000 labour hours
	8450 units should take	16,900 hours
	So 900 × £2.75 is	£2475 F

58 Exam Practice Kit: Fundamentals of Management Accounting

    (iii) Capacity

Actual hours worked	16,600
Budgeted hours	16,000
600 more so 600 × £2.75 =	£1650 F

    (iiii) Efficiency

8450 units should take	16900 hours
8450 units did take	16600 hours
So 300 × £2.75 =	£825 F

Note

Capacity + Efficiency =	Volume
£1650 + £825 =	£2475

6.8 Material variances

Material price

2250 kg should have cost	£22500
2250 kg did cost	£20500
So £2000 F	

Material usage

1,000 units should have used	2,000 kg
1,000 units did use	2,250 kg
So 250 × £10 =	£2250

6.9   (i) The material usage variance, being favourable, indicates that the amount of material used was less than expected for the actual output achieved. This could be caused by the purchase of higher quality materials, which resulted in less wastage than normal.

  (ii) The labour rate variance, being favourable, indicates that the hourly wage rate paid was lower than expected. This could be due to employing a lower grade employee than was anticipated in the budget.

  (iii) The sales volume contribution variance, being adverse, indicates that the number of units sold was less than budgeted. This may have been caused by the increased sales price of £11 (compared to a budgeted price of £10) which has reduced customer demand, or due to the actions of competitors.

6.10 Interdependence of variances is the term used to describe the situation when there is a single cause of a number of variances.

For example, the use of a higher grade of labour than was anticipated is likely to cause an adverse labour rate variance, a favourable labour efficiency variance, and possibly a favourable material usage variance (due to more experience of working with materials).

It is important that when variances are reported, the possibility that some of them may have a common cause should be acknowledged, and managers encouraged to work together for the benefit of the organisation.

Multiple choice questions

Questions 6.1 to 6.7 are based on the following budgeted and actual figures for XYZ Ltd in the latest financial year.

Budget

Sales	50,000 units at £100
Production	55,000 units
Materials	110,000 kg at £20 per kg
Labour	82,500 hours at £2 per hour
Variable overhead	82,500 hours at £6 per hour

Actual

Sales	53,000 units at £95
Production	56,000 units
Materials purchased	130,000 kg
Opening inventory of materials	0
Closing inventory of materials	20,000 kg
Materials purchase price	£2,700,000
Labour	85,000 hours paid at £180,000
Labour	83,000 hours worked
Variable overhead	£502,000

6.1 The sales price variance was

    A   £265,000 (A)
    B   £265,000 (F)
    C   £99,000 (A)
    D   £99,000 (F)

6.2 The sales volume contribution variance was

    A   £144,000 (F)
    B   £48,000 (F)
    C   £300,000 (F)
    D   £100,000 (F)

6.3 The materials usage variance was

    A   £20,000 (A)
    B   £20,000 (F)
    C   £40,000 (A)
    D   £40,000 (F)

6.4 The idle time variance was

    A   £2,000 (F)
    B   £2,000 (A)
    C   £4,000 (F)
    D   £4,000 (A)

6.5 The labour efficiency variance was

   A £4,000 (F)
   B £4,000 (A)
   C £2,000 (F)
   D £2,000 (A)

6.6 The variable overhead expenditure variance was

   A £2,000 (F)
   B £2,000 (A)
   C £4,000 (F)
   D £4,000 (A)

6.7 The variable overhead efficiency variance was

   A £6,000 (A)
   B £6,000 (F)
   C £4,000 (A)
   D £4,000 (F)

6.8 During the latest period the number of labour hours worked was 1,000. The wages paid amounted to £14,500 and the labour rate variance was £1,300 adverse. The standard labour rate per hour was:

   A £11.15
   B £13.20
   C £14.50
   D £15.80

6.9 Which of the following is a possible cause of an adverse labour efficiency variance?

   A The original standard time was set too high
   B The employees were more skilled than had been planned for in the standard
   C Production volume was lower than budgeted
   D An ideal standard was used for labour time

6.10 The following data have been recorded for employee no. 763 last period:

Number of hours worked	82
Number of units produced	40
Standard time allowed per unit	2.25 hours
Bonus payable at basic hourly rate	30% of time saved
Basic hourly rate of pay	£11

The gross wages payable to the employee for the period are:

   A £902.00
   B £904.40
   C £928.40
   D £990.00

✓ Multiple choice solutions

6.1 **A**

Sales price variance
53,000 × £5 = £265,000 (A)
Actual price below budget.

6.2 **A**

Standard contribution per unit:

	£ per unit
Sales price	100
Materials (110,000 × £20)/55,000	(40)
Labour (82,500 × £2)/55,000	(3)
Variable overhead (82,500 × £6)/55,000	(9)
Contribution	48

The sales volume contribution variance
3,000 × £48 = £144,000 (F)

6.3 **D**

Materials usage variance

Standard usage (56,000 × 2)	112,000 kg
Actual usage	110,000

Used 2,000 kg less than expected at £20 per kg so £40,000 (F).

6.4 **D**

Idle time variance is difference between hours paid and hours worked × hourly rate. It is always negative or adverse.

Actual hours paid	85,000
Actual hours worked	83,000
Idle time 2,000 × £2	
So £4,000 (A).	

6.5 **C**

Labour efficiency is the difference between standard time allowed and actual hours.

Standard time (56,000 × 1.5 hours)	84,000 hours
Actual time	83,000 hours
Labour efficiency rate (1,000 × £2)	£2,000 (F)

62 Exam Practice Kit: Fundamentals of Management Accounting

6.6 **D**

Standard rate × actual hours (£6 × 83,000) = £498,000
Actual variable overhead expenditure = £502,000
Variable overhead expenditure variance 4,000 (A)

6.7 **B**

Variable overhead efficiency variance

Same hours as labour Question 6.5
1,000 × £6 = £6,000 (F)

6.8 **B**

Wages paid	£14,500
Rate variance	£1,300 (A)
Standard rate for hours worked	£13,200

Standard rate per hour = £13,200/1,000 = £13.20.

6.9 **D**

An ideal standard makes no allowances for stoppages or idle time therefore it is most likely to result in an adverse labour efficiency variance.

If the original standard time was set too high then the labour efficiency variance would be favourable. Employees who are more skilled are likely to work faster than standard, again resulting in a favourable efficiency variance. The efficiency variance is based on the expected time for the actual production volume therefore it is not affected by a difference between budgeted and actual production volume.

6.10 **C**

Standard time for units produced (40 × 2.25)	90	hours
Actual time taken	82	hours
Time saved	8	hours

Bonus payable (30% × 8 hours × £11)	£26.40
Basic wage (82 hours × £11)	£902.00
Gross wages payable	£928.40

7

Cost Book-keeping

Cost Book-keeping 7

? Concepts and definitions questions

7.1 What are integrated accounts?

7.2 State six accounts in a manufacturing business which will contain control accounts.

(i)
(ii)
(iii)
(iv)
(v)
(vi)

Questions 7.3–7.5 are based on the following information:

NB Ltd operates an integrated accounting system. At the beginning of October, the following balances appeared in the trial balance:

	£'000	£'000	£'000
Freehold buildings		800	
Plant and equipment, at cost		480	
Provision for depreciation on plant and equipment			100
Inventories:			
Raw materials		400	
Work-in-process 1:			
Direct materials	71		
Direct wages	50		
Production overhead	<u>125</u>	246	
Work-in-process 2:			
Direct materials	127		
Direct wages	70		
Production overhead	<u>105</u>	302	
Finished goods		60	
Receivables		1,120	
Capital			2,200
Profit retained			220
Payables			300
Bank			464
Sales			1,200
Cost of sales		888	
Abnormal loss		9	
Production overhead under/over absorbed			21
Administration overhead		120	
Selling and distribution overhead		<u>80</u>	
		<u>4,505</u>	<u>4,505</u>

The transactions during the month of October were

	£'000
Raw materials purchased on credit	210
Raw materials returned to suppliers	10
Raw materials issued to	
Process 1	136
Process 2	44
Direct wages incurred	
Process 1	84
Process 2	130
Direct wages paid	200
Production salaries paid	170
Production expenses paid	250
Received from customers	1,140
Paid to suppliers	330
Administration overhead paid	108
Selling and distribution overhead paid	84
Sales on credit	1,100
Cost of goods sold	844

	Direct materials £'000	Direct wages £'000
Abnormal loss		
Process 1	6	4
Process 2	18	6
Transfer from process 1 to process 2	154	94
Transfer from process 2 to finished goods	558	140

Plant and equipment is depreciated at the rate of 20% per annum, using the straight-line basis. Production overhead is absorbed on the basis of direct wages cost.

7.3   What are the production overhead absorption rates for process 1 and for process 2?

7.4   Write up the ledger accounts.

7.5   A company operates an integrated cost and financial accounting system. If an issue of direct materials to production was requisitioned what would the accounting entries be?

68 Exam Practice Kit: Fundamentals of Management Accounting

✓ Concepts and definitions solutions

7.1 Integrated accounts are a set of accounting records which provide both financial and cost accounts using a common input of data for all accounting purposes.

7.2 Control accounts

   (i) Stores
   (ii) WIP
   (iii) Finished goods
   (iv) Production overhead
   (v) Administration costs
   (vi) Marketing costs.

7.3 Process 1

$$\text{Overhead absorbed rate (OAR)} = \frac{\text{Budgeted overheads}}{\text{Budgeted level of activity}}$$

$$= \frac{£125,000}{£50,000} = 250\% \text{ of direct labour cost}$$

(from work-in-process figures)

Process 2

$$\text{OAR} = \frac{£105,000}{£70,000} = 150\% \text{ of direct labour cost}$$

7.4

Freehold buildings at cost

	£'000		£'000
Bal b/f	800		

Plant and equipment

	£'000		£'000
Bal b/f	480		

Provision for depreciation on plant and equipment

	£'000		£'000
Bal c/f	108		100
		Production overhead control (W1)	8
	108		108
		Bal b/f	108

Raw materials

	£'000		£'000
Bal b/f	400	Payables	10
Payables	210	Work-in-process 1	136
		Work-in-process 2	44
		Bal c/f	420
	610		610
Bal b/f	420		

Work-in-process 1

	£'000		£'000
Bal b/f	246	Abnormal loss (W3)	20
Raw materials	136	Work-in-process 2 (W2)	483
Wages	84	Bal c/f	173
Production overhead control (W4)	210		
	676		676
Bal b/f	173		

Work-in-process 2

	£'000		£'000
Bal b/f	302	Abnormal loss (W6)	33
Raw materials	44	Finished goods (W7)	908
Wages	130	Bal c/f	213
Work-in-process 1 (W2)	483		
Production overhead control (W5)	195		
	1,154		1,154
Bal b/f	213		

Finished goods

	£'000		£'000
Bal b/f	60	Cost of sales	844
Work-in-process 2 (W7)	908	Bal c/f	124
	968		968
Bal b/f	124		

Receivables

	£'000		£'000
Bal b/f	1,120	Bank	1,140
Sales	1,100	Bal c/f	1,080
	2,220		2,220
Bal b/f	1,080		

Capital

	£'000		£'000
		Bal b/f	2,200

Profit retained

	£'000		£'000
		Bal b/f	220

Payables

	£'000		£'000
Raw materials	10	Bal b/f	300
Bank	330	Raw materials	210
Bal c/f	170		
	510		510
		Bal b/f	170

Bank

	£'000		£'000
Receivables	1,140	Bal b/f	464
Bal c/f	466	Wages	200
		Production overhead control	170
		Production overhead control	250
		Payables	330
		Administration overhead	108
		Selling and distribution overhead	84
	1,606		1,606
		Bal b/f	466

Sales

	£'000		£'000
Bal c/f	2,300	Bal b/f	1,200
		Receivables	1,100
	2,300		2,300
		Bal b/f	2,300

Cost of sales

	£'000		£'000
Bal b/f	888	Bal c/f	1,732
Finished goods	844		
	1,732		1,732
Bal b/f	1,732		

Abnormal loss

	£'000		£'000
Bal b/f	9	Bal c/f	62
Work-in-process 1 (W3)	20		
Work-in-process 2 (W6)	33		
	62		62
Bal b/f	62		

Production overhead under/over absorbed

	£'000		£'000
Production overhead control	23	Bal b/f	21
		Bal c/f	2
	23		23
Bal b/f	2		

Administration overhead

	£'000		£'000
Bal b/f	120	Bal c/f	228
Bank	108		
	228		228
Bal b/f	228		

Selling and distribution overhead

	£'000		£'000
Bal b/f	80	Bal c/f	164
Bank	84		
	164		164
Bal b/f	164		

Wages

	£'000		£'000
Bank	200	Work-in-process 1	84
Bal c/f	14	Work-in-process 2	130
	214		214
		Bal b/f	14

Production overhead control

	£'000		£'000
Bank	170	Work-in-process 1 (W4)	210
Bank	250	Work-in-process 2 (W5)	195
Depreciation (W1)	8	Under absorption	23
	428		428

Workings

1. Depreciation = 20% × £480,000 × 1/12 = £8,000
2. Transfer from process 1 to process 2 = materials £154,000 + wages £94,000 + overheads £(94,000 × 250%) = £483,000
3. Value of abnormal loss in process 1 = materials £6,000 + wages £4,000 + overheads £(4,000 × 250%) = £20,000
4. Production overhead absorbed in process 1 = £84,000 × 250% = £210,000
5. Production overhead absorbed in process 2 = £130,000 × 150% = £195,000
6. Value of abnormal loss in process 2 = materials £18,000 + wages £6,000 + overheads £(6,000 × 150%) = £33,000
7. Value of transfer from process 2 to finished goods = materials £558,000 + wages £140,000 + overheads £(140,000 × 150%) = £908,000

7.5 The accounting entries for an issue of direct materials to production would be

Debit WIP since this increases the asset, and credit stores control since this decreases the asset materials inventory.

Multiple choice questions

7.1 A firm operates an integrated cost and financial accounting system. The accounting entries for an issue of direct materials to production would be

    A DR WIP control account
        CR stores control account
    B DR finished goods account
        CR stores control account
    C DR stores control account
        CR WIP control account
    D DR cost of sales account
        CR WIP control account

7.2 In an integrated cost and financial accounting system, the accounting entries for factory overhead absorbed would be:

    A DR WIP control account
        CR overhead control account
    B DR overhead control account
        CR WIP account
    C DR overhead control account
        CR cost of sales account
    D DR cost of sales account
        CR overhead control accounts

7.3 The book-keeping entries in a standard cost system when the actual price for raw materials is less than the standard price are

    A DR raw materials control account
        CR raw materials price variance account
    B DR WIP control account
        CR raw materials control account
    C DR raw materials price variance account
        CR raw materials control account
    D DR WIP control account
        CR raw materials price variance account

7.4 A company uses standard costing and an integrated accounting system.

The accounting entries for an adverse labour efficiency variance are

    A Debit WIP control account
        Credit labour efficiency variance account
    B Debit labour efficiency variance account
        Credit WIP control account
    C Debit wages control account
        Credit labour efficiency variance account
    D Debit labour efficiency variance account
        Credit wages control account

7.5 At the end of the period the accounting entries for production overhead over-absorbed would be:

A   DR Overhead control account
    CR Income statement
B   DR Income statement
    CR Overhead control account
C   DR Work in progress account
    CR Overhead control account
D   DR Overhead control account
    CR Work in progress account

7.6 In an integrated system the accounting entries for the issue of indirect production materials would be:

A   DR Production overhead control account
    CR Work in progress account
B   DR Work in progress account
    CR Production overhead control account
C   DR Production overhead control account
    CR Stores control account
D   DR Stores control account
    CR Production overhead control account

7.7 In an integrated standard costing system the accounting entries for an adverse labour rate variance would be:

A   DR Labour rate variance account
    CR Work in progress account
B   DR Work in progress account
    CR Labour rate variance account
C   DR Labour rate variance account
    CR Wages control account
D   DR Wages control account
    CR Labour rate variance account

7.8 A record of total actual expenditure incurred on indirect costs and the amount absorbed into individual units, jobs or processes is known as:

A   Production Overhead Control Account
B   Production Overabsorption Account
C   Production Underabsorption Account
D   Work-in-Progress Account

7.9 When materials are purchased on credit, what would be the relevant cost bookkeeping entry?

A   Debit Work-in-Progress
    Credit Materials
B   Debit Materials
    Credit Accounts Payable

C   Debit Materials
    Credit Work-in-Progress
D   Debit Cost of Sales
    Credit Materials

7.10 Consider the following incomplete data:

1. Work-in-Progress wages   £30,000
2. Production overhead   £40,000
3. Transfer to finished goods £350,000
4. Closing inventory   £75,000

What was the value of raw materials brought into production?

A   £325,000
B   £350,000
C   £355,000
D   £375,000

☑ Multiple choice solutions

7.1 A

The entry would be DR work-in-progress control account and CR stores control account.

7.2 A

In an integrated cost and financial accounting system, the accounting entries for factory overhead absorbed would be

DR WIP control account

CR overhead control account.

7.3 A

The book-keeping entries in a standard cost system when the actual price for raw materials is less than the standard price are

DR Raw materials control account

CR Raw materials price variance account.

7.4 B

A company which found that they had an adverse labour efficiency variance should

Debit labour efficiency variance account

Credit WIP control account.

7.5 A

Over-absorbed overhead is transferred from the overhead control account as a credit in the income statement.

7.6 C

Indirect production costs, such as the cost of indirect materials, are collected in the debit side of the production overhead control account pending their later absorption into work in progress.

7.7 C

An adverse variance is debited in the relevant variance account. This eliminates options B and D. The variance arose at the point of payment of the wages therefore the credit entry is made in the wages control account.

7.8 A

This is known as Production Overhead Control Account.

7.9 B

Debit Materials

Credit Accounts Payable

7.10 **C**

WIP Control Account:

Wages	£30,000	Finished goods	£350,000
Production	£40,000	Closing inventory	£75,000
Raw materials	£355,000		
	----------		----------
	£425,000		£425,000

The raw materials is the balancing figure of £355,000.

8

Job and Batch Costing

Job and Batch Costing

8

Concepts and definitions questions

8.1 What is job costing?

8.2 State four items which would appear on a job cost sheet:

(i)
(ii)
(iii)
(iv)

8.3 What is batch costing?

8.4 When products are made in batches for inventory, the quantity to be produced will be determined by:

(i)
(ii)
(iii)
(iv)

8.5 Company A bases its estimates on the following formula:

Total cost = Prime cost + 40% overhead
Selling price = Total cost + 25% profit
Estimates for two jobs show

	Job X £	Job Y £
Direct materials	200	100
Direct wages £5 per hour	500	600
Prime cost	700	700

Calculate the selling price of each job. Is this the best way to absorb overhead?

8.6 State three discrepancies which could appear between a job cost card and the financial accounts:

(i)
(ii)
(iii)

Questions 8.7–8.9 are based on the following information:

A company specialises in printing advertising leaflets and is in the process of preparing its price list. The most popular requirement is for a folded leaflet made from a single sheet of A4 paper. From past records and budgeted figures, the following data have been estimated for a typical batch of 10,000 leaflets.

Artwork £65
Machine setting 4 hours at £22 per hour
Paper £12.50 per 1,000 sheets
Ink and consumables £40
Printers' wages 4 hours at £8 per hour
General fixed overheads are £15,000 per period during which a total of 600 labour hours are expected to be worked.
The firm wishes to achieve 30% profit on sales.

8.7 Calculate the selling price per thousand leaflets for quantities of 10,000 and 20,000 leaflets.

8.8 Calculate the profit for the period if 64 batches of 10,000 and 36 batches of 20,000 were sold and costs and revenues were as budgeted.

8.9 Comment on the results achieved in the period.

8.10 What is the collective term for job, batch and contract costing and what are their distinguishing features?

✓ Concepts and definitions solutions

8.1 Job costing is a form of specific order costing in which costs are attributed to individual jobs.

8.2 Four items which would appear on a job cost sheet are

   (i) Materials purchased specifically for the job
   (ii) Materials drawn from inventory
   (iii) Direct wages
   (iv) Direct expenses.

8.3 Batch costing is a form of specific order costing in which costs are attributed to batches of products.

8.4 Batch determination

   When products are made in batches for inventory, the batch size will be determined by:

   (i) The rate of consumption
   (ii) Storage costs
   (iii) Time required to take down and set up production facilities
   (iv) Capacity available in relation to other requirements of the company.

8.5 Job costing worked example

	Job X £	Job Y £
Direct materials	200	100
Direct wages	500	600
Add: 40% overhead	280	280
Add: 25% of total cost	245	245
Selling price	£1,225	£1,225

Whatever method is chosen for absorbing overhead, there will be an argument to use another method. In job Y, direct wages were higher which would indicate that more workers were used on this job or the same number of workers took longer. So if overhead was based on labour hours, job Y should have been more expensive than job X.

8.6 Discrepancies between job cost card and financial accounts

   (i) Material requisition on job card not recorded
   (ii) Direct labour shown as indirect
   (iii) Over/under absorption of various overheads.

8.7 Batch costing worked example

	Produces 10,000 £	Produces 20,000 £
Artwork	65	65
Machine setting (4 × 22)	88	88
Paper (12.50 × 10) (12.50 × 20)	125	250
Ink and consumables	40	80
Printers wages (4 × 8) (8 × 8)	32	64
	350	547
Fixed overheads absorbed £25 per labour hour	100	200
Total cost	450	747
Profit 30% $\left(\frac{3}{7} \times 450\right)\left(\frac{3}{7} \times 747\right)$	193	320
Selling price	643	1,067
Selling price per 1,000	£64	£53

8.8 Profit for the period

	£
Revenue from 10,000 (64 × £64 × 10)	40,960
Revenue from 20,000 (36 × £53 × 20)	38,160
	79,120
Direct costs 10,000 (64 × £350)	22,400
Direct costs 20,000 (36 × £547)	19,692
	42,092
Fixed overheads	15,000
	57,092

Profit = £79,120 − £57,092 = £22,028

8.9 Comment on results

(i) Actual hours worked (64 × 4) + (36 × 8) = 544
(ii) Budgeted hours 600
(iii) 56 hours of excess capacity
(iv) Find more 10,000 leaflet jobs to fill capacity since profit per labour hour is higher.

$$10{,}000 \text{ leaflet job} = \frac{£640 \times 30\%}{4} = £48$$

$$20{,}000 \text{ leaflet job} = \frac{£1{,}060 \times 30\%}{8} = £39.75$$

8.10
The collective term for job, batch and contract costing is specific order costing. The distinguishing features are:

(i) Work is separated as opposed to a continuous flow
(ii) Work can be identified with a particular customer's order

Multiple choice questions

8.1 Which of the following are contained in a typical job cost?

(i) Actual material cost
(ii) Actual manufacturing overheads
(iii) Absorbed manufacturing overheads
(iv) Actual labour cost

A   (i), (ii) and (iv)
B   (i) and (iv)
C   (i), (iii) and (iv)
D   (i), (ii), (iii) and (iv)

Questions 8.2–8.5 are based on this scenario:

A printing and publishing company has been asked to provide an estimate for the production of 100,000 programmes for the Cup Final 64 pages (32 sheets of paper)

There are four operations in the setup.

1 *Photography* – Each page requires a photographic session costing £150 per session.
2 *Setup costs* – A plate is required for each page. Each plate requires 4 hours of labour at £7 per hour and £35 of materials. Overheads are absorbed at £9.50 per labour hour.
3 *Printing* – Paper costs £12 per 1,000 sheets. Wastage is expected to be 2% of input. Other costs are £7 per 500 programmes and 1,000 programmes are printed per hour of machine time. Overheads are absorbed in printing at £62 per machine hour.
4 *Binding* – These costs are recovered at £43 per hour and 2,500 programmes can be bound in an hour. Profit margin of 10% selling price is needed.

8.2 The printing costs for the job are

A   £44,721
B   £45,632
C   £46,784
D   £47,520

8.3 The total cost for the job is

A   £64,568
B   £65,692
C   £66,318
D   £67,474

8.4 The selling price of a programme is

A   70p
B   71p
C   72p
D   75p

8.5 What would be the additional costs charged to the job, if the labour efficiency ratio achieved versus estimate in setup is 90%?

A £423.80
B £446.20
C £469.30
D £487.10

The following data are to be used for Questions 8.6 and 8.7 below:

A firm uses job costing and recovers overheads on direct labour cost.

Three jobs were worked on during a period, the details of which were

	Job 1 £	Job 2 £	Job 3 £
Opening work-in-progress	8,500	0	46,000
Material in period	17,150	29,025	0
Labour for period	12,500	23,000	4,500

The overheads for the period were exactly as budgeted £140,000.

Jobs 1 and 2 were the only incomplete jobs.

8.6 What was the value of closing work-in-progress?

A £81,900
B £90,175
C £140,675
D £214,425

8.7 Job 3 was completed during the period and consisted of 2,400 identical circuit boards. The firm adds 50% to total production costs to arrive at a selling price.

What is the selling price of a circuit board?

A It cannot be calculated without more information
B £31.56
C £41.41
D £58.33

The following data are to be used for the Questions 8.8–8.10:

A firm makes special assemblies to customers' orders and uses job costing. The data for a period are

	Job number AA10 £	Job number BB15 £	Job number CC20 £
Opening WIP	26,800	42,790	0
Material added in period	17,275	0	18,500
Labour for period	14,500	3,500	24,600

The budgeted overheads for the period were £126,000

8.8 How much overhead should be added to job number CC20 for the period?

   A   £24,600
   B   £65,157
   C   £72,761
   D   £126,000

8.9 Job number BB15 was completed and delivered during the period and the firm wishes to earn 33 1/3 % profit on sales.

   What is the selling price of job number BB15?

   A   £69,435
   B   £75,521
   C   £84,963
   D   £138,870

8.10 What was the approximate value of closing WIP at the end of the period for job number AA10 and CC20?

   A   £58,575
   B   £101,675
   C   £147,965
   D   £217,323

88 Exam Practice Kit: Fundamentals of Management Accounting

✓ Multiple choice solutions

8.1 **C**

Overhead cost is absorbed into job costs using a pre-determined absorption rate. It is not usually possible to identify the actual manufacturing overhead costs related to specific jobs.

8.2 **C**

Printing costs

	£
Paper $\left(\dfrac{100{,}000 \times 32}{1{,}000} \times £12 \div 0.98\right)$	39,184
Other costs $\left(\dfrac{100{,}000 \times £7}{500}\right)$	1,400
Machine hours (100 × £62)	6,200
	46,784

8.3 **A**

Total costs

		£
1 Photography (64 × £150)		9,600
2 Set up	£	
Labour (64 × 4 × £7)	1,792	
Materials (64 × £35)	2,240	
Overhead (256 × £9.50)	2,432	
		6,464
3 Printing (as per Question 8.2)		46,784
4 Binding (40 × £43)		1,720
		64,568

8.4 **C**

$$\text{Selling price} = \dfrac{£64{,}568}{0.9} = \dfrac{£71{,}742}{100{,}000} = 72 \text{ pence}$$

8.5 **C**

Estimated setup hours = 256

$$\dfrac{256}{0.9} = 284.4 \text{ hours}$$

Additional costs (284.4 − 256) × £16.50 = £469.30

Job and Batch Costing **89**

8.6 **D**

	Job 1 £	Job 2 £	Total £
Opening WIP	8,500	–	8,500
Materials	17,150	29,025	46,175
Labour	12,500	23,000	35,500
Overheads	43,750	80,500	124,250
	81,900	132,525	214,425

Total labour for period = £(12,500 + 23,000 + 4,500) = £40,000

Overhead absorption rate = $\dfrac{£140,000}{£40,000}$ = 350% of labour cost

8.7 **C**

	Job 3 £
Opening WIP	46,000
Labour	4,500
Overheads (3.5 × £4,500)	15,750
Total production costs	66,250
Profit 50%	33,125
Selling price of 2,400	99,375
Selling price per unit	£41.41

8.8 **C**

Overhead absorption

$\dfrac{24,600}{24,600 + 14,500 + 3,500} \times £126,000 = £72,761$

8.9 **C**

	£
WIP	42,790
Materials	–
Labour	3,500
Overhead $\left(\dfrac{3,500}{24,600 + 14,500 + 3,500} \times £126,000\right)$	10,352
	56,642

Sales price = $\dfrac{£56,642}{66^2/_3} \times 100 = £84,963$

8.10 **D**

	AA10 £	CC20 £	Total £
Opening WIP	26,800	–	
Materials	17,275	18,500	
Labour	14,500	24,600	
Overhead	42,887	72,761	
Total	101,462	115,861	217,323

9

Contract Costing

Contract Costing 9

❓ Concepts and definitions questions

9.1 What is contract costing?

9.2 In contract costing, each contract is a separately identifiable cost unit. Which costs would be included in such an account?

   (i)
   (ii)
   (iii)
   (iv)

9.3 What is the relationship between architects' certificates and retention money?

9.4 When we calculate an interim profit in contract costing what are the five steps that need to be taken?

   (i) *Step 1*
   (ii) *Step 2*
   (iii) *Step 3*
   (iv) *Step 4*
   (v) *Step 5*

Questions 9.5–9.8 are based on the following information:

Contract 815 commenced during Year 5 and has a fixed contract price of £250,000. The costs incurred during Year 5 for materials, wages and sub-contractors charges were £120,000. Plant costing £25,000 was purchased during Year 5 specifically for contract 815.

At the end of Year 5:

   (i) Plant was valued at £20,000
   (ii) Unused materials on the site were valued at £20,000
   (iii) Architects' certificates had been issued showing that the value of work completed was £100,000.

94 Exam Practice Kit: Fundamentals of Management Accounting

It is estimated that further costs totalling £75,000 would be incurred in order to complete the job.

Retention money representing 20% of the certified value of the work completed has been held back. The balance has been paid. The contractor credits the contract account with the full value of the architects' certificates as they are received.

9.5   Calculate the total estimated contract costs.

9.6   Calculate the contract profit.

9.7   Calculate the profit to be taken in Year 5.

9.8   Write up the ledger account for contract number 815

Questions 9.9 and 9.10 are based on the following data:

GUF Fencing Ltd has a contract for security perimeter fencing with a premier league football club.

Work is part complete at the year end 31st December Year 5. George, his accountant, does not understand contract accounting but he is a meticulous book-keeper and has kept the following information:

		£'000
Contract price		3,000
Direct materials issued	680	
Returned to suppliers	30	
Transferred to other jobs	30	
On site at 31/12	75	
Direct wages		
Paid	450	
Accrued	20	
Direct expenses		
Paid	75	
Accrued	25	
Value of work certified		
to date		1,600
Received from client		1,200
Plant installed on site at cost		200
Depreciation to 31/12		50
Estimated cost to complete		800

Progress payments are based on architects' certificates less 25% retention.

9.9   Calculate attributable profit for the year to December Year 5.

9.10 Prepare the contract and client ledger accounts.

✅ Concepts and definitions solutions

9.1 Contract costing is a form of specific order costing in which costs are attributed to individual contracts.

9.2 Contract cost accounting

Costs to be included:

(i) Direct materials
(ii) Direct wages
(iii) Direct expenses
(iv) Indirect costs.

9.3 Architects' certificates and retention money

As the work on a contract proceeds, the client's architect will issue a certificate which indicates that so much of a contract has been completed and that the contractor is due to be paid a certain amount of money. This is known as an architect's certificate.

Normally the contractor would receive a proportion of this figure, since some of the money would be held back by the client. This is to ensure that any faults have been rectified before any final payment is due. This is known as retention money.

9.4 Calculation of interim profit

Step 1 – Determine the total sales value of the contract.

Step 2 – Compute the total expected costs to complete the contract. This will consist of:

(i) The actual costs incurred to date
(ii) The estimated future costs necessary to complete the contract

Step 3 – The expected overall contract profit

= Step 1 – Step 2

Step 4 – Calculate the attributable profit to date

$$= \frac{\text{Value of certified work to date}}{\text{Total sales value of contract}} \times \text{expected overall profit}$$

Step 5 – The profit to be taken this year is the cumulative attributable profit calculated at Step 4 less than any profit which has been taken on previous years.

9.5 Calculation of contract costs

Actual costs incurred to date

	£
Materials, wages and subcontractors	120,000
Less: Materials on site at end Year 5	(20,000)
	100,000
Plant depreciation (£25,000 − £20,000)	5,000
Contract costs incurred to end Year 5	105,000
Add: Estimated future costs to complete contract	75,000
So total estimated contract costs	180,000

9.6 Contract profit

	£
Fixed contract price	250,000
Less: Contract costs	180,000
Contract profit (est)	70,000

9.7 Profit to be taken in Year 5

$$\frac{\text{Work certified}}{\text{Contract price}} \times \text{estimated contract profit}$$

$$= \frac{£100,000}{£250,000} \times £70,000$$

$$= £28,000$$

9.8 Contract number 815

	£		£
Materials, wages and subcontractors	120,000	Work certified	100,000
		Materials c/d	20,000
Plant at cost	25,000	Plant c/d	20,000
Income statement	28,000	WIP c/d	33,000
	173,000		173,000

9.9 Further worked example

Actual costs incurred to date

	£'000	£'000
Materials issued		680
Less: Returns	30	
Transferred to other jobs	30	
On site 31/12	75	(135)
		545
Wages paid and accrued		470
Direct expenses paid and accrued		100
Plant depreciation		50
Contracts costs incurred to date		1,165

Contract costs to completion	£'000
Incurred	1,165
Estimated future costs	800
Total estimated contract costs	1,965
Fixed contract price	3,000
Total estimated costs	1,965
Estimated profit	1,035

$$\text{Attributable profit} = \frac{\text{Work certified}}{\text{Contract price}} \times \text{contract profit}$$

$$= \frac{1,600}{3,000} \times £21,035,000$$

$$= £552,000$$

9.10

Contract account

	£'000		£'000
Material issued	680	Material returns	30
Wages		Transfer	30
Cash	450	Work certified	1,600
Accrued	20	Plant c/d	150
Direct expenses		Materials c/d	75
Paid	75	WIP c/d	117
Accrued	25		
Plant	200		
Income statement	552		
	2002		2002

Client contractee account

	£'000		£'000
Contract account		Cash received	1,200
Certified work	1,600	Balance c/d	400
	1,600		1,600

Multiple choice questions

Questions 9.1–9.3 are concerned with the following information about a contract:

	£'000
Costs incurred to date	2,860
Costs estimated to complete contract	3,920
Value of work certified to date	3,310
Total value of contract	7,100

9.1 What is the total expected contract profit?

   A £300,000
   B £320,000
   C £340,000
   D £360,000

9.2 Calculate the attributable profit using costs as a measure of completion.

   A £134,985
   B £135,870
   C £136,250
   D £137,580

9.3 Attributable profit using sales value as a measure of completion is

   A £149,183
   B £150,571
   C £151,432
   D £152,237

9.4 A construction company has the following data concerning one of its contracts.

	£m
Contract price	2.00
Value certified	1.30
Cash received	1.20
Costs incurred	1.05
Cost of work certified	1.00

The company estimates the attributable profit on contracts based on the proportion of the value of work certified that has been paid by the client.

The profit to be attributed to the contract is

   A £272,485
   B £274,586
   C £276,923
   D £280,410

9.5 Which one of the following is not a contract cost?

   A Direct wages
   B Depreciation of plant

C Sub-contractors' fees
D Architects' certificates

9.6 The attributable profit to date on a contract should reflect the amount of work that has been completed so far. It can be calculated as follows:

A $\dfrac{\text{Value of work certified to date}}{\text{Total sales value of contract}} \times \text{expected profit}$

B $\dfrac{\text{Total sales value of contract}}{\text{Value of work certified to date}} \times \text{expected profit}$

C $\dfrac{\text{Value of work certified to date}}{\text{Total sales value of contract}} \div \text{expected profit}$

D $\dfrac{\text{Total sales value of contract}}{\text{Value of work certified to date}} - \text{expected profit}$

9.7 State which of the following are characteristics of contract costing.

(i) Homogenous products
(ii) Customer-driven production
(iii) Short timescale from commencement to completion of the cost unit

A (i) and (ii)
B (ii) and (iii)
C (i) and (iii)
D (ii) only

9.8 Which industries would use contract costing?

(i) Construction
(ii) Civil engineering
(iii) Financial services
(iv) Motor industry

A (i) and (ii)
B (ii) and (iii)
C (iii) and (iv)
D (i), (ii) and (iv)

9.9 The cost of any sub-contracted work is

A A direct expense of a contract and is debited to the contract account
B An indirect expense of a contract and is debited to the contract account
C A direct expense of a contract and is debited to the client account
D An indirect expense of a contract and is debited to the client account

9.10 Progress payments received by the contractor from the client are

A Debited to the contract account
B Credited to the contract account
C Debited to the client account
D Credited to the client account

✓ Multiple choice solutions

9.1 B

Contract profit

	£'000
Contract value	7,100
Costs incurred	(2,860)
Costs to complete	(3,920)
So expected profit	£320,000

9.2 A

Using costs

$$\frac{2,860}{6,780} \times £320,000 = £134,985$$

9.3 A

Using value

$$\frac{\text{Value certified}}{\text{Total sales value}} \times £320,000$$

$$= \frac{3,310}{7,100} \times £320,000 = £149,183$$

9.4 C

	£ m
Value certified	1.3
Cost of work certified	1.0
	0.3

So $£300,000 \times \dfrac{\text{cash received}}{\text{value certified}}$

$$= \frac{£300,000 \times £1.2 \text{ million}}{£1.3 \text{ million}}$$

$= £276,923$

9.5 D

Architects' certificates – they are concerned with payments.

9.6 A

The attributable profit can be calculated using the formula:

$$\frac{\text{Value of work certified to date} \times \text{expected profit}}{\text{Total sales value of contract}}$$

9.7 D

The only characteristic of contract costing mentioned is that it is customer-driven production.

9.8 **A**

Construction and civil engineering would be industries which use contract costing, since most jobs would carry on into another financial year.

9.9 **A**

The cost of any sub-contracted work is a direct expense of a contract and is debited to the contract account.

9.10 **D**

Progress payments received by the contractor are credited to the client account.

10

Process Costing

Process Costing 10

? Concepts and definitions questions

10.1 What is process costing and when is it applied?

10.2 What is a normal loss?

10.3 Calculate the cost per tonne from the following data:

	£
Input 5,000 tonnes	20,000
Labour cost	8,000
Overhead	5,000

Normal loss is 10% of input and has a scrap value of £3 per tonne.

Write up the process account and the normal loss account.

10.4 Distinguish between an abnormal loss and an abnormal gain.

10.5 Calculate the net cost/profit of the abnormal loss/gain from the following data:

Input quantity	5,000 kg at £5 per kg
Normal loss	10%
Process costs	£17,490
Actual output	4,200 kg

Losses are sold for £2 per kg.

10.6 A manufacturer starts a process on 1st January. In the month of January, he starts work on 20,000 units of production. At the end of the month there are 5,000 units still in process which are 75% complete. Costs for the period were £20,625.

Calculate:

(i) The value of completed units at the end of January
(ii) The value of WIP at the end of January

10.7 What are the six step methods for process costing?

(i) Step 1
(ii) Step 2
(iii) Step 3
(iv) Step 4
(v) Step 5
(vi) Step 6

Questions 10.8–10.10 are based on the following information:

C Ltd manufactures a range of products and the data below refer to one product which goes through one process only. The company operates a 13 four-weekly reporting system for process and product costs and the data given below relate to Period 10.

There was no opening work in progress.

5,000 units of materials input at £2.94 per unit entered the process.

	£
Further direct materials added	13,830
Direct wages incurred	6,555
Production overhead	7,470

Normal loss is 3% of input.

Closing WIP was 800 units but these were incomplete, having reached the following percentages of completion for each of the elements of cost listed:

	%
Direct materials added	75
Direct wages	50
Production overhead	25

270 units were scrapped after a quality control check when the units were at the following degrees of completion.

	%
Direct materials added	66⅔
Direct wages	33⅓
Production overhead	16⅔

Units scrapped, regardless of the degree of completion, are sold for £1 each and it is company policy to credit the process account with the scrap value of normal loss units.

10.8 Prepare the Period 10 process account.

10.9 Prepare the abnormal gain or loss account.

10.10 Suggest two causes of

(i) Abnormal loss
(ii) Abnormal gain

✓ Concepts and definitions solutions

10.1 Process costing applies when goods result from a sequence of continuous or repetitive operations or processes. It can be found in brewing, oil refining and food processing.

10.2 A normal loss is the amount of loss that is expected from the operation of a process. This loss is expected and is based on past experience and is also considered unavoidable.

10.3 Process and normal loss account

Process account

	Tonnes	£		Tonnes	Price/Tonne	£
Materials	5,000	20,000	Normal loss	500	3	1,500
Labour cost		8,000	Output	4500	7	31,500
Overhead		5,000				
	5,000	33,000		5,000		33,000

$$\text{Cost per tonne of good output} = \frac{\text{total costs} - \text{scrap sales}}{\text{Expected output}} = \frac{33,000 - 1,500}{4,500}$$

$$£ = 7/\text{tonne}$$

Normal loss account

	Tonnes	£		Tonnes	£
Process account	500	1,500	Cash/bank	500	1,500

10.4 Abnormal loss and abnormal gain

The extent to which the actual loss exceeds the normal loss is referred to as the abnormal loss.

An abnormal gain is where the normal loss is less than expected, for example, if material input was 1,000 kgs and normal loss was 10%, if actual output was 950 kgs there would be an abnormal gain of 50 kgs and if actual output was 875 kgs then there would be an abnormal loss of 25 kgs.

10.5

Process account

	kg	£		kg	£	£
Materials	5,000	25,000	Normal loss	500	2.00	1,000
Process costs		17,490	Output	4,200	9.22	38,724
			Abnormal loss	300	9.22	2,766
	5,000	42,490		5,000		42,490

$$\text{Cost of good output} = \frac{42,490 - 1,000}{4,500} = £9.22/\text{kg}$$

Net cost is therefore £9.22 − £2.00 = £7.22/kg

300 × £7.22 = £2,166

Abnormal loss account

	kg	£		kg	£
Process a/c	300	2,766	Cash/bank		600
			Income statement		2,166

10.6

	Units	Percentage completion	Equivalent units
Started and completed	15,000	100%	15,000
Work-in-process	5,000	75%	3,750
			18,750

Cost per equivalent unit = $\dfrac{£20,625}{18,750}$ = £1.10

Value of completed units = 15,000 × £1.10 = £16,500

Value of WIP = 3,750 × £1.10 = £4,125

10.7 Six step methods for process costing

Step 1 – Trace the physical flow of units so that units input to the production process are reconciled with units output or in process at the end of the period.

Step 2 – Convert the physical units determined in Step 1 into equivalent units of production for each cost element.

Step 3 – Calculate the total cost for each cost element for the period.

Step 4 – Divide the total costs by equivalent units to establish a cost per equivalent unit.

Step 5 – Multiply equivalent units by the cost per equivalent unit to cost out finished production and work-in-process.

Step 6 – Write up ledger accounts.

10.8

Process account

	Units	£		Units	£
Input	5,000	14,700	Normal loss	150	150
Direct materials		13,830	Closing WIP (W1)	800	5,160
Direct wages		6,555	Abnormal loss (W1)	120	696
Production overhead		7,470	Output (W1)	3,930	36,549
	5,000	42,555		5,000	42,555

(W1) Equivalent units table

	Total	%	Input EU	%	Material added EU	%	Wages EU	%	Ohd EU
Normal loss	150	0	–	0	–	0	–	0	–
Closing WIP	800	100	800	75	600	50	400	25	200
Abnormal loss	120	100	120	66⅔	80	33⅓	40	16⅔	20
Output	3,930	100	3,930	100	3,930	100	3,930	100	3,930
	5,000		4,850		4,610		4,370		4,150

	£	£	£	£
Costs	14,700	13,830	6,555	7,470
Normal loss scrap value	(150)			
	£14,550	£13,830	£6,555	£7,470

Cost/equivalent unit = $\frac{14,550}{4,850}$ $\frac{13,830}{4,610}$ $\frac{6,555}{4,370}$ $\frac{7,470}{4,150}$

= £3 = £3 = £1.50 = £1.80

(W1)
Value of output = 3,930 × (3 + 3 + 1.5 + 1.8) = 236,549
Value of WIP = (800 × 3) + (600 × 3) + (400 × 1.5) + (200 × 1.8) = £5,160
Value of abnormal loss = (120 × 3) + (80 × 3) + (40 × 1.5) + (20 × 1.8) = £696

10.9 **Abnormal loss account**

	£		£
Process	696	Scrap	120
		Income statement	576
	696		696

10.10 The abnormal loss could have resulted from the use of poorer quality materials than normal or from inexperienced employees operating the process wrongly.

Abnormal gain could come from higher grade materials and higher grade labour.

Multiple choice questions

Questions 10.1–10.3 are based on the following information:

Input quantity   1,000 kg
Normal loss   10% of input
Process costs   £14,300
Actual output   880 kg
Losses are sold for £8 per kg

10.1   Normal loss is equal to

      A   10 kg
      B   50 kg
      C   100 kg
      D   120 kg

10.2   The cost per unit is equal to

      A   £10
      B   £15
      C   £20
      D   £25

10.3   The impact on the income statement as a result of the abnormal loss would be

      A   £120
      B   £130
      C   £140
      D   £150

Questions 10.4–10.9 are based on the following extracts:

Process A
Direct material   2,000 kg at £5 per kg
Direct labour   £7,200
Process plant time   140 hours at £60 per hour

Process B
Direct material   1,400 kg at £12 per kg
Direct labour   £4,200
Process plant time   80 hours at £72.50 per hour

The department overhead for the period was £6,840 and is absorbed into the costs of each process on direct labour cost. Output from Process A is input into Process B.

	Process A	Process B
Expected output was	80% of input	90% of input
Actual output was	1,400 kg	2,620 kg

There is no finished goods inventory at the beginning of the period and no WIP at either the beginning or the end of the period.

Losses are sold for scrap for 50p per kg from process A and £1.825 per kg from process B.

Process Costing 111

10.4 The departmental overhead absorption rate is what percentage of direct labour costs?

    A 40%
    B 45%
    C 55%
    D 60%

10.5 The cost per kg of process A is equal to

    A £15.62
    B £16.73
    C £18.58
    D £19.62

10.6 The cost per kg of process B is equal to

    A £20.50
    B £21.25
    C £21.75
    D £22.25

10.7 The abnormal loss in process A is

    A 100 kg
    B 200 kg
    C 300 kg
    D 400 kg

10.8 The abnormal gain in process B is

    A 100 kg
    B 200 kg
    C 300 kg
    D 400 kg

10.9 The value of the finished goods at the end of process B is

    A £55,235
    B £56,329
    C £56,567
    D £56,985

10.10 The following details relate to the main process of X Ltd, a chemical manufacturer.

Opening WIP

2,000 litres fully completed as to materials and 40% complete as to conversion.

Material input   24,000
Normal loss is 10% of input
Output to process 2   19,500 litres

Closing WIP

3,000 litres fully completed as to materials and 45% complete as to conversion.

The numbers of equivalent units to be included in X Ltd's calculation of the cost per equivalent unit, using a weighted average basis of valuation are

	Materials	Conversion
A	21,400	20,850
B	22,500	21,950
C	22,500	20,850
D	23,600	21,950

✅ Multiple choice solutions

10.1 C

Normal loss is equal to 10% of 1,000 kg = 100 kgs

10.2 B

The cost per unit	£
Process costs	14,300
Less: Normal loss scrap	800
	13,500

$$\text{Cost per unit} = \frac{£13{,}500}{900}$$

$$= £15$$

10.3 C

	£
Abnormal loss cost (20 × £15)	300
Less: Scrap value (20 × £8)	160
	140

10.4 D

$$\text{Departmental overhead absorption rate} = \frac{£6{,}840}{£7{,}200 + £4{,}200}$$

$$= 60\% \text{ of direct labour cost}$$

10.5 C

Process A

$$\text{Cost/kg} = \frac{\text{Total cost} - \text{scrap value of normal loss}}{\text{Expected output}}$$

Total costs

	£
Direct materials (2,000 kg × £5)	10,000
Direct labour	7,200
Process plant time (140 hours × £60)	8,400
Departmental overhead	4,320
	29,920
Less: Scrap value of normal loss (20% × 2,000 × £0.50)	200
	29,720

$$\text{Cost per kg} = \frac{£29,720}{1,600 \text{ kg}}$$

$$= £18.575/\text{kg}$$

So C to nearest pence.

10.6   **C**

Process B

	£
Process A (1,400 kg × £18.575)	26,005
Direct labour	4,200
Direct materials (1,400 kg × £12)	16,800
Process plant time (80 × £72.50)	5,800
Departmental overhead	2,520
	55,325
Less: Scrap value of normal loss (2,800 kg × 10% × £1.825)	511
	54,814

$$\text{Cost per kg} = \frac{£54,814}{2,520}$$

$$= £21.75/\text{kg}$$

10.7   **B**

	kg	Process A		kg
Input	2,000	Process B		1,400
		Normal loss		400
		Abnormal loss		200
	2,000			2,000

10.8   **A**

Process B

	kg		kg
Input from process A	1,400	Normal loss	280
Direct materials	1,400	Finished goods	2,620
Abnormal gain	100		
	2,900		2,900

Abnormal gain = 100 kg

10.9   **D**

Value of finished goods = 2,620 × £21.75
                       = £56,985

10.10 **D**

Process account

	litres		litres
Opening WIP	2,000	Normal loss	2,400
Input	24,000	Output	19,500
		Closing WIP	3,000
		Abnormal loss	1,100
	26,000		26,000

Equivalent units table

	Materials		*Conversion*	
	%	EU	%	EU
Output	100	19,500	100	19,500
Abnormal loss	100	1,100	100	1,100
Closing WIP	100	3,000	45	1,350
		23,600		21,950

11

Managerial Reports in a Service Organisation

Managerial Reports in a Service Organisation   11

Concepts and definitions questions

11.1 What is service costing?

11.2 State three industries where service costing can be applied.

   (i)
   (ii)
   (iii)

11.3 Cost units for service industries

   Match the following cost units with the following services:

Service	Cost unit
Restaurants	Passenger miles
Carriers	Patient days
Hospitals	Tonne-miles
Passenger transport	Meals served

11.4 State four differences between a service industry and a manufacturing industry.

   (i)
   (ii)
   (iii)
   (iv)

11.5 State three differences between a manufacturing and a service cost statement.

   (i)
   (ii)
   (iii)

11.6   What is a composite cost unit?

Questions 11.7–11.10 are based on the following scenario:

George and Helen have recently set up their own auditing practice. They have agreed to take a salary of £20,000 per annum in their first year of trading. They have purchased two cars at £13,000 each and expect to use them for three years. At the end of three years, the cars have an expected resale value of £4,000. Straight line depreciation is to be used.

Each expects to work for 8 hours per day, 5 days per week and for 45 weeks per year. They refer to this as available time.

Around 25% of available time is expected to be dealing with administration matters related to their own business and in the first year there will be an idle time of 22.5% of available time. The remainder of available time is expected to be charged to clients.

They agree that their fees should be based on:

(i)   An hourly rate for productive client work
(ii) An hourly rate for travelling to/from clients
(iii) Rate per mile travelled to/from clients

They expect that the travelling time will equal 25% of their chargeable time and will cover 18,000 miles.

This time should be charged at 1/3 of their hourly rate.

Other costs include

	£
Electricity	1,200
Fuel for vehicles	1,800
Insurance – office	600
Insurance – vehicles	800
Mobile telephone	1,200
Office rent and rates	8,400
Office telephone	1,800
Postage	500
Secretarial costs	8,400
Vehicle repairs	1,200
Vehicle road tax	280

11.7   The hourly rate for client work was £

11.8   The hourly rate for travelling to/from clients was £

11.9   The rate per mile travelled to/from clients was £

11.10   What method of cost accounting was used in the last three examples?

Managerial Reports in a Service Organisation

✅ Concepts and definitions solutions

11.1 Service costing is the cost accounting method that can be applied when the business provides a service or a service function within a manufacturing company.

11.2 Industries using service costing

    (i)   Road haulage
    (ii) Hotels
    (iii) Hospitals

11.3

Service	*Cost unit*
Restaurants	Meals served
Carriers	Tonne-miles
Hospitals	Patient days
Passenger transport	Passenger miles

11.4 Differences between service and manufacturing industry

    (i)   *Intangibility*: Output takes the form of performance, for example, a waiter in a restaurant rather than some tangible good.
    (ii) *Heterogeneity*: The standard of service industries is variable due to large human input.
    (iii) *Simultaneous production and consumption*: Service industries do not have the luxury of storing their product; it is produced and consumed simultaneously.
    (iv) *Perishability*: Related to (iii) – if an airline takes off with excess capacity that revenue is then lost forever.

11.5 Manufacturing and service cost statement

The major differences between a manufacturing and a service cost statement are

    (i)   In the service sector there is a lack of detailed variance analysis.
    (ii) Inventory figures in service industries will be low in relation to turnover.
    (iii) Service industries have their own performance measures, for example, hotels occupancy rates.

11.6 Composite cost unit

A major problem for service industries is to decide a suitable unit to measure the service. Composite cost units take into account a number of factors, for example, in the road haulage industry, tonne miles travelled takes into account not only the distance travelled but also the weight carried.

Workings for Questions 11.7–11.10

	Professional services (£)	Vehicles (£)
Salaries	40,000	
Car depreciation		6,000
Electricity	1,200	
Fuel		1,800
Insurance		
Office	600	
Vehicles		800
Telephone		
Mobile	1,200	
Office	1,800	
Office rent + rates	8,400	
Postage	500	
Secretarial	8,400	
Vehicle services		1,200
Road tax		280
	62,100	10,080

	Hours
Hours available (2 × 8 × 5 × 45)	3,600
Administration 25%	(900)
Idle time 22.5%	(810)
Chargeable time	1,890
Travel time 25%	472.5
Active time	1,417.5

Effective chargeable hours	
Travel time (472.5 × 1/3)	157.50
+ active time (1,417.5 × 1)	1,417.50
	1,575

11.7 Hourly rate for client work

$$\frac{£62,100}{1,575} = £39.43 \text{ per hour}$$

11.8 Travel $= \dfrac{£39.43}{3} = £13.14$

11.9 Vehicle rate per mile $= \dfrac{£10,080}{18,000}$
= 56p per mile

11.10 The method of costing in the last three examples is service costing.

Multiple choice questions

11.1 For a company operating a fleet of delivery vehicles, which of the following would be most useful?

   A   Cost per mile
   B   Cost per driver hour
   C   Cost per tonne mile
   D   Cost per tonne carried

11.2 Which of the following are characteristics of service costing?

   (i)   High levels of indirect costs as a proportion of total cost
   (ii) Use of composite cost units
   (iii) Use of equivalent units

   A   (i) only
   B   (i) and (ii)
   C   (ii) only
   D   (ii) and (iii)

11.3 Which of the following is not an example of a composite cost unit?

   A   Kilowatt hours
   B   Meals served
   C   Patient days
   D   Tonne miles

11.4 Which of the following would be regarded as a fixed cost of a commercial transport fleet?

   (i)   Road fund licence
   (ii) Insurance
   (iii) Diesel
   (iv) Maintenance

   A   (i) and (ii)
   B   (i) and (iii)
   C   (ii) and (iii)
   D   (ii) and (iv)

11.5 Which of the following are key differences between the products of service industries and those of manufacturing businesses?

   (i)   Intangibility
   (ii) Perishability
   (iii) Heterogeneity
   (iv) Simultaneous production and consumption

   A   (i) and (ii)
   B   (i), (ii) and (iii)
   C   (i), (ii) and (iv)
   D   (i), (ii), (iii) and (iv)

124 Exam Practice Kit: Fundamentals of Management Accounting

Questions 11.6 and 11.7 are based on the following information:

A company specialises in carrying out tests on animals to see if they have any infection. At present the laboratory carries out 12,000 tests per annum but has the capacity to test a further 6,000 if required.

The current cost of carrying out a trial test is

	£ per test
Materials	115
Technician's fees	30
Variable overhead	12
Fixed overhead	50

To increase capacity to 18,000 it would:

- require a 50% shift premium on technician's fees
- enable a 20% discount to be obtained on materials
- increase fixed costs by £700,000

The current fee per test is £300

11.6 The level of profit based on 12,000 tests is

    A   £1,116,000
    B   £132,000
    C   £1,164,000
    D   £1,192,000

11.7 How much would profit be, if 18,000 tests were carried out?

    A   £1,492,000
    B   £1,525,000
    C   £1,598,000
    D   £1,610,000

Questions 11.8, 11.9 and 11.10 are based on the following information:

A transport company has three divisions and you are given the following data.

	Division A	Division B	Division C
Sales (£'000)	200	300	250
No. of vehicles	50	20	10
Distance travelled ('000 km)	150	100	50
Identifiable fixed costs	25	30	35

Variable costs are £300,000 for the company as a whole and are estimated to be in the ratio of 1:4:5 respectively for A, B and C.

The fixed costs which are not directly identifiable are £75,000. These are shared equally between the three divisions

11.8 The contribution of division A was

    A   £120,000
    B   £145,000
    C   £170,000
    D   £180,000

11.9 The contribution per kilometre of division B was

    A £1.25
    B £1.40
    C £1.50
    D £1.80

11.10 The total net profit of the three divisions was

    A £240,000
    B £285,000
    C £325,000
    D £375,000

126 Exam Practice Kit: Fundamentals of Management Accounting

✓ Multiple choice solutions

11.1 C

The most useful measure would be cost per tonne mile since it measures both distance and amount carried.

11.2 B

Alternatives (i) and (ii) are valid Equivalent units as used in process costing.

11.3 B

The odd one out is meals served since this only takes into account one factor.

11.4 A

Road fund licence and insurance costs are costs which are not based on activity.

Diesel and maintenance would be classified as variable costs. Maintenance costs at the very least are semi-variable costs.

11.5 D

Intangibility, perishability, heterogeneity and simultaneous production and consumption are all features of service industry and are therefore different from manufacturing industry.

11.6 A

12,000 capacity

	£'000	£'000
Fees (12,000 × £300)		3,600
Variable costs		
Materials (12,000 × £115)	1,380	
Wages (12,000 × £30)	360	
Variable overhead (12,000 × £12)	144	
		1,884
Contribution		1,716
Fixed overhead (12,000 × £50)		600
Profit		1,116

11.7 C

18,000 tests

	£'000	£'000
Fees (18,000 × £300)		5,400
Variable costs		
Materials (18,000 × £115 × 80%)	1,656	
Wages (360 + (6 × 30 × 150%))	630	
Variable overhead (144 × 150%)	216	
		2,502
Contribution		2,898
Fixed overhead		1,300
		1,598

Workings for Questions 11.8, 11.9 and 11.10

	Division A	Division B	Division C
	£ 000	£ 000	£ 000
Sales	200	300	250
Variable costs	30	120	150
Contribution	170	180	100
Identifiable fixed costs	25	30	35
Other fixed costs	25	25	25
Profit	120	125	40

11.8 **C**

Division A = Sales − variable cost

= £200,000 − £30,000 = £170,000

11.9 **D**

Division B

Total contribution £180,000
Distance travelled 100,000 km

Contribution per km = £1.80

11.10 **B**

Total net profit = £120,000 + £125,000 + £40,000 = £285,000.

12

Functional Budgets

Functional Budgets   12

❓ Concepts and definitions questions

12.1 State six aims of budgeting.

   (i)
   (ii)
   (iii)
   (iv)
   (v)
   (vi)

12.2 What is a budget?

12.3 State seven items that might be included in a budget manual.

   (i)
   (ii)
   (iii)
   (iv)
   (v)
   (vi)

12.4 The production budget needs to be translated into requirements for:

   (i)
   (ii)
   (iii)
   (iv)

12.5 What is a budget centre?

12.6 What is the difference between a budget and a forecast?

12.7 Consider the following budgeted figures:

Sales	£450,000
Opening inventory	£20,000
Closing inventory	£30,000
Raw materials	£120,000
Direct labour	£130,000
Production overhead	£120,000
Administration	£45,000

What is the budgeted operating profit for the period?

12.8 Name six types of functional budgets.

(i)
(ii)
(iii)
(iv)
(v)
(vi)

12.9 State five functions of a budget committee.

(i)
(ii)
(iii)
(iv)
(v)

12.10 What is the principal budget factor?

✓ Concepts and definitions solutions

12.1 Aims of budgeting

  (i) Planning and co-ordination
  (ii) Authorising and delegating
  (iii) Evaluating performance
  (iv) Discerning trends
  (v) To communicate and motivate
  (vi) To control.

12.2 A budget may be defined as a quantitative statement, for a defined period of time which may include planned revenues, expenses, assets, liabilities and cash flows. It provides a focus for the organisation and is part of the strategic process.

12.3 Items that might be included in a budget manual

  (i) An explanation of the budgetary planning and control process
  (ii) An organisation chart to show budget responsibilities
  (iii) A timetable for budget preparation
  (iv) Copies of any forms to be completed by budget holders
  (v) The organisation's account codes
  (vi) Key assumptions to be made in the planning process
  (vii) Name and location of the budget officer

12.4 Production budget
Required for:

  (i) Raw materials
  (ii) Direct labour
  (iii) Machine hours
  (iv) Production overheads

12.5 Budget centre

A budget centre is a section in an organisation for which control may be exercised and budgets prepared.

12.6 Budget and forecast

A forecast is a prediction of what is expected to happen, a budget is a quantified, formal plan that the organisation is aiming to achieve.

12.7 Master budget income statement

	£	£
Sales		450,000
Cost of sales		
Opening inventory	20,000	
Raw materials	120,000	
Direct labour	130,000	
Production overhead	120,000	
	390,000	
Closing inventory	30,000	360,000
Operating margin		90,000
Administration		45,000
Operating profit		45,000

12.8 Types of functional budgets

(i) Sales
(ii) Production
(iii) Purchasing
(iv) Research and development
(v) Human resource management
(vi) Logistics.

12.9 Budget committee

A budget committee would normally comprise of the chief executive, the management accountant and functional heads.

The functions of these committees are to

(i) Agree overall policy objectives with regard to the budget
(ii) Co-ordinate budgets
(iii) Suggest amendments to budgets
(iv) Improve budgets
(v) Examine budgeted and actual results.

12.10

The principal budget factor is the limiting factor since this determines all other budgets.

In most companies, the level of demand determines the size and scale of the operation which is why many budgetary planning processes begin with the sales budget.

Multiple choice questions

Questions 12.1–12.6 are based on the following data.

Loxo sells office equipment and is preparing his budget for next month.

	Opening inventory	Budgeted sales	Selling price
	Units	Units	£ per unit
BAX	63	290	120
DAX	36	120	208
FAX	90	230	51

Closing inventory is 30% of sales units for the month.

All three products are made using Material A, Material B, Labour Grade C and Labour Grade D.

The quantities are as follows:

	Material A	Material B	Labour C	Labour D
	Metres	Cubic metres	Hours	Hours
BAX	4	2	3	2
DAX	5	3	5	8
FAX	2	1	2	–
Cost	£12 per metre	£7 per cubic metres	£4 per hour	£6 per hour

Loxo's opening inventory of Material A is 142 metres and 81 cubic metres of Material B. He intends to increase this during April, so that there is sufficient raw materials to produce 50 units of each item of equipment.

12.1 Budgeted sales revenues for the period were

    A £71,440
    B £71,490
    C £72,360
    D £72,490

12.2 The budgeted production of FAX's during the month was

    A 203 units
    B 207 units
    C 209 units
    D 219 units

12.3 The budgeted wage of material A during the month was

    A 2,000 metres
    B 2,144 metres
    C 2,220 metres
    D 2,274 metres

12.4 The budgeted cost of labour for the month was

   A £16,960
   B £17,368
   C £18,415
   D £19,314

12.5 Budgeted purchases of material A during the month were:

   A £27,288
   B £32,184
   C £34,162
   D £35,586

12.6 The budgeted gross profit for the period was

   A £19,200
   B £19,300
   C £19,600
   D £19,700

12.7 When preparing a production budget the quantity produced equals

   A Sales + opening inventory + closing inventory
   B Sales + opening inventory − closing inventory
   C Sales − opening inventory + closing inventory
   D Sales − opening inventory − closing inventory

12.8 The principal budget factor is

   A The highest value item of cost
   B A factor common to all budget centres
   C The limiting factor
   D A factor known by the budget centre manager

12.9 Which is the last budget to be prepared in the master budget?

   A Sales budget
   B Cash budget
   C Budgeted income statement
   D Budgeted balance sheet

12.10 What is budget slack?

   A Additional time built into the planning process to ensure that all budgets are prepared according to the timetable
   B Additional revenue built into the sales budget to motivate the sales team
   C Additional costs built into an expenditure budget to guard against overspending
   D Spare machine capacity that is not budgeted to be utilised

✓ Multiple choice solutions

12.1 B

Budgeted sales

BAX (290 × £120)	£34,800
DAX (120 × £208)	£24,960
FAX (230 × £51)	£11,730
	£71,490

12.2 C

	FAX Units
Sales	230
Closing inventory	69 (30%)
	299
Opening inventory	90 (given)
Production	209

12.3 D

Material used is based on production

	Metres
BAX (314 × 4)	1,256
DAX (120 × 5)	600
FAX (209 × 2)	418
	2,274

12.4 B

Labour C		Labour D	
	Hours		Hours
(314 × 3)	942	(314 × 2)	628
(120 × 5)	600	(120 × 8)	960
(209 × 2)	418		–
	1,960		1,588

So, (1,960 × £4) + (1,588 × £6)
= £7,840 + £9,528
= £17,368

12.5 **B**

	Metres
Materials used	2,274

See Question 12.3 for workings of the materials used figure

Closing inventory 50 × (4 + 5 + 2)
Enough to produce 50 units of each   550
                                        2,824

Opening inventory (given)   (142)
                                   2,682

Therefore, 2,682 × £12 = £32,184.

12.6 **D**

Unit cost

	BAX £	DAX £	FAX £
Material A	48	60	24
Material B	14	21	7
Labour C	12	20	8
Labour D	12	48	–
	86	149	39

	£
BAX (290 × £(120 − 86))	9,860
DAX (120 × £(208 − 149))	7,080
FAX (230 × £(51 − 39))	2,760
	19,700

12.7 **C**

Production budget

Sales − opening inventory + closing inventory.

12.8 **C**

The principal budget factor is the limiting factor.

12.9 **D**

The last budget to be prepared in the master budget is the budgeted balance sheet.

12.10 **C**

Budget slack is the intentional overestimating of costs or underestimating of revenues to ensure that the budget is achievable.

13

Cash Budgets

Cash Budgets

13

❓ Concepts and definitions questions

13.1 What is a cash budget?

13.2 What are the objectives of a cash budget?

13.3 What are the six stages in the preparation of a cash budget?

(i)
(ii)
(iii)
(iv)
(v)
(vi)

13.4 The budgeted sales for a company during the first three months of next year are as follows:

	January £	February £	March £
Sales	500	600	800

All sales are on credit, and customers tend to pay as follows:

	%
In month of sale	10
In month after sale	40
Two months after sale	45

Bad debt is 5% of sales. How much cash is collected in March?

Questions 13.5–13.7 are based on the following budgeted data:

	January Units	February Units	March Units
Opening inventory	100	150	120
Closing inventory	150	120	180
Sales	400	450	420

141

The cost of inventory is £5 per unit and 50% of purchases are paid in cash and 50% are paid on credit, two months after the purchase.

13.5 Calculate the budgeted purchases in units for February.

13.6 How many units were budgeted to be purchased over the three-month period?

13.7 How much was budgeted to be paid to suppliers during March?

13.8 What is a spreadsheet?

13.9 State three things which are stored in a spreadsheet.

13.10 What is "what if" analysis?

Concepts and definitions solutions

13.1 A cash budget is a detailed budget of cash inflows and outflows covering both revenue and capital items.

13.2 Objectives of a cash budget

The objectives of a cash budget are to anticipate any shortages/surpluses and to provide management information in short- and medium-term cash planning and in planning for longer-term finance for the organisation.

13.3 Stages in a cash budget

  (i) Forecast sales revenue
  (ii) Forecast time lag in converting receivables to cash
  (iii) Determine inventory levels, therefore purchasing requirements
  (iv) Forecast time lag on paying suppliers
  (v) Incorporate other cash payments and receipts
  (vi) Collate all this cash flow information to determine the net cash flows.

13.4 Cash collected in March

	£
March sales 10% of 800	80
Feb sales 40% of 600	240
Jan sales 45% of 500	225
	545

13.5 Purchases in February (units)

Sales	450
Opening inventory	(150)
Closing inventory	120
Purchases in units	420

13.6 Three months purchases

Purchases in January

	Units
Sales	400
Opening inventory	(100)
Closing inventory	150
	450

Purchases in February (see Question 13.5) 420 units

Purchases in March

	Units
Sales	420
Opening inventory	(120)
Closing inventory	180
	480

So, 450 + 420 + 480 = 1,350 units

13.7 Amount paid to suppliers in March
50% of March purchases + 50% of January purchases
= (50% × 480 units × £5) + (50% × 450 units × £5)
= £2,325

13.8 A spreadsheet is a computer package which stores data in a matrix format where the intersection of each row and column is referred to as cell.

13.9 Cell storage

Each cell within a spreadsheet can be used to store

(i) A label
(ii) A value
(iii) A formula.

13.10 "What if" analysis

Final budgets are dependent on the values entered for sales units and the like. Alterations will be made before the final budget is drawn up. The use of a spreadsheet allows these changes to be made accurately and quickly using formulae. Such an exercise is known as "what if" analysis.

Multiple choice questions

13.1 Of the four costs shown below, which one would not be included in the cash budget of a greengrocer?

   A   Petrol for the van
   B   Depreciation of the van
   C   Shop assistants wages
   D   Payments made to suppliers

13.2 The budgeted sales for an organisation are as follows:

	January	February	March	April
Sales	£600	£800	£400	£500

These are all credit sales and customers tend to pay in the following pattern:
15% in month of sale
35% in month after sale
42% two months after sale
Bad debts 8% of sales

How much cash would the firm expect to collect in March?

   A   £540
   B   £551
   C   £592
   D   £600

13.3 A sole trader is preparing a cash budget for January. His credit sales are

Actual	October	£80,000
	November	£60,000
	December	£100,000

Estimated January £50,000.

His recent debt collection experience is

	%
Current month's sales	20
Prior month's sales	60
Sales two months prior	10
Cash discounts taken for payment in the current month	5
Bad debts	5

How much may he expect to collect in January?

   A   £70,500
   B   £75,500
   C   £76,000
   D   £80,000

13.4 A partnership are preparing their cash budget for September with the following credit sales:

June	£42,460
July	£45,640
August	£47,980
September	£49,480

Recent experience suggests that 60% of customers pay in the month after sale, 25% in month 2, 12% in month 3 with 3% bad debt.

Customers paying in the month after sale are entitled to a 2% discount.

How much cash (to the nearest £) would be collected from credit sales in September?

A £44,717
B £45,725
C £46,372
D £47,639

Questions 13.5–13.7 are based on the following budgeted information:

	October Units	November Units	December Units
Opening inventory	100	120	150
Closing inventory	120	150	130
Sales	500	450	520

The cost of inventory stock is £10 per unit with 40% of purchases for cash, 30% paid in the month after purchase and 30% paid two months after purchase.

13.5 The budgeted number of units to be purchased in November was

A 440
B 480
C 520
D 560

13.6 The value of purchases in October were budgeted to be

A £4,400
B £4,800
C £5,200
D £5,600

13.7 The amount paid to suppliers in December was budgeted to be

A £5,000
B £6,000
C £7,000
D £8,000

13.8 A master budget compromises

　　A　The budgeted income statement
　　B　The budgeted cash flow, budgeted income statement and budgeted balance sheet
　　C　The budgeted cash flow
　　D　The capital expenditure budget

13.9 A company is currently preparing its cash budget for next year. The sales budget is as follows:

	£
March	60,000
April	70,000
May	55,000
June	65,000

40% of its sales are expected to be for cash. Of its credit sales, 70% are expected to pay in the month after sale and take a 2% discount. 27% are expected to pay in the second month after the sale, and the remaining 3% are expected to be bad debts.

The value of sales receipts to be shown in the cash budget for May is

　　A　£58,491
　　B　£59,546
　　C　£60,532
　　D　£61,475

13.10 Purchases are budgeted to be

	£
January	56,000
February	77,000
March	68,000
April	74,000

The company pays invoices in the month following receipt. In the master budgets for the three months ended 30th April the total payment for purchases shown in the cash budget will

　　A　Be higher than the total purchases shown in the income statement.
　　B　Be lower than the total purchases shown in the income statement.
　　C　Be the same as the total purchases shown in the income statement.
　　D　Be the same as the trade payables shown in the balance sheet.

148 Exam Practice Kit: Fundamentals of Management Accounting

✅ Multiple choice solutions

13.1 B

Petrol, wages and payments made to suppliers could all appear on a cash budget. Odd one out is depreciation, where no cash changes hands.

13.2 C

	£
March sales (15% × £400)	60
February sales (35% × £800)	280
January sales (42% × £600)	252
	592

13.3 B

Cash in January

	£
Jan sales (20% × 95% × £50,000)	9,500
Dec sales (60% × £100,000)	60,000
Nov sales (10% × £60,000)	6,000
	75,500

13.4 A

Cash collected in September

	£
August (£47,980 × 98% × 60%)	28,212.24
July (£45,640 × 25%)	11,410.00
June (£42,460 × 12%)	5,095.20
	44,717.24

13.5 B

Purchases in November

	Units
Sales	450
Opening inventory	(120)
Closing inventory	150
	480

13.6 C

Purchases in October

	Units
Sales	500
Opening inventory	(100)
Closing inventory	120
Purchases	520

So, 520 × £10 = £5,200.

13.7 A

Payment to suppliers (December)

	£
December purchases (40% × 500 × £10)	2,000
November purchases (30% × 480 × £10)	1,440
October purchases (30% × 520 × £10)	1,560
	5,000

13.8 B

A master budget comprises the budgeted cash flow, budgeted income statement and budgeted balance sheet.

13.9 C

Cash received in May

	£
May sales (40% × £55,000)	22,000
April sales (60% × 70% × 98% × £70,000)	28,812
March sales (60% × 27% × £60,000)	9,720
	60,532

13.10 B

Cash payments shown in cash budget are

January	£56,000
February	£77,000
March	£68,000
	£201,000

Purchases shown in the income statement

February	£77,000
March	£68,000
April	£74,000
	£219,000

14

Flexible Budgets

Flexible Budgets 14

❓ Concepts and definitions questions

14.1 What is a flexible budget?

14.2 State two advantages and two disadvantages of a flexible budget.

Advantages

 (i)
 (ii)

Disadvantages

 (i)
 (ii)

14.3 What is a volume variance?

14.4 What is an expenditure variance?

14.5 What is a flexed budget?

154 Exam Practice Kit: Fundamentals of Management Accounting

✓ Concepts and definitions solutions

14.1 A flexible budget is a budget which, by recognising different cost behaviour patterns, is designed to change as volume of activity changes.

14.2 *Advantages*

(i) Fixed budgets make no distinction between fixed and variable costs.
(ii) Fixed budgets take no account of production shortfall.

Disadvantages

(i) Flexible budgets are more expensive to operate.
(ii) In many businesses, especially service industries, most costs are fixed over a budget period.

14.3 Volume variance

A volume variance is the difference in costs and revenues caused by a difference between the planned level of activity and the actual level of activity.

14.4 Expenditure variance

An expenditure variance is the difference between the budgeted level of expenditure for the actual level of activity and the actual level of expenditure.

14.5 Flexed budget

An original budget is set at the beginning of the period based on the estimated level of activity. This is, then, flexed to correspond with the actual level of activity.

Consider the following example.

A company manufactures a single product but activity levels vary widely from month to month. The budgeted figures are based on an average activity level of 10,000 units of production each month.

The actual figures for last month are also shown:

	Budget £	Actual £
Direct labour	10,000	9,400
Materials	5,000	4,800
Variable overhead	5,000	4,300
Depreciation	10,000	10,000
Fixed overhead	5,000	5,200
	35,000	33,700
Production	10,000	9,500

	Flexed	Actual	Variance
Production units	9,500	9,500	
	£	£	£
Direct labour	9,500	9,400	100 (F)
Materials	4,750	4,800	50 (A)
Variable overhead	4,750	4,300	450 (F)
Depreciation	10,000	10,000	–
Fixed overhead	5,000	5,200	200 (A)
	34,000	33,700	300 (F)

Multiple choice questions

14.1 Actual output is 162,500 units
 Actual fixed costs (as budgeted) £87,000
 Actual expenditure £300,000
 Over budget by £18,000 (based on a flexible budget comparison)

The budgeted variable cost per unit is

A 80p
B £1.00
C £1.20
D £1.31

14.2 The budgeted variable cost per unit was £2.75. When output was 18,000 units, total expenditure was £98,000. Fixed overheads were £11,000 over budget, variable costs were the same as budget. The amount budgeted for fixed cost was

A £30,000
B £34,250
C £36,750
D £37,500

Questions 14.3–14.5 are based on the following data:

	Budget	Actual
Production	20,000 units	17,600 units
Direct labour	£20,000	£19,540
Variable overhead	£4,200	£3,660
Depreciation	£10,000	£10,000

14.3 The direct labour variance was

A £17,600 (A)
B £19,540 (A)
C £1,940 (A)
D £1,940 (F)

14.4 The variable overhead variance was

A £3,960 (F)
B £3,660 (F)
C £72 (F)
D £36 (F)

14.5 If volume variance is £5,400F and expenditure variance is £2,400A, the total variance is

A £3,000F
B £3,000A
C £7,800F
D £7,800A

14.6 Variable costs are conventionally deemed to

   A   Be constant per unit of output
   B   Vary per unit of output as production volume changes
   C   Be constant in total when production volume changes
   D   Vary in total, from period to period when production is constant

14.7 A flexible budget is

   A   A budget of variable production costs only.
   B   A budget which is updated with actual costs and revenues as they occur during the budget period.
   C   A budget which shows the costs and revenues at different levels of activity.
   D   A budget which is prepared for a period of six months and reviewed monthly. Following such a review, a further one month's budget is prepared.

14.8 Which of the following is a criticism of fixed budgets?

   A   They make no distinction between fixed and variable costs.
   B   They provide a formal planning framework that ensures planning does take place.
   C   They co-ordinate the various separate aspects of the business by providing a master plan.
   D   They provide a framework of reference within which later operating decisions can be taken.

14.9 In January a company produced 1,200 units at a cost of £9,800.

   In February they produced 1,000 units at a cost of £8,700.

   If March production is expected to be 1,250 units, what should be the budgeted cost?

   A   £10,000
   B   £10,025
   C   £10,075
   D   £11,025

14.10 The difference between the flexed budget and the actual results is known as the:

   A   Volume variance
   B   Expenditure variance
   C   Price variance
   D   Capacity variance

✓ Multiple choice solutions

14.1 C

Budgeted expenditure	£282,000
Less: Fixed costs	£87,000
Total variable costs	£195,000

$$\text{Variable cost per unit} = \frac{£195,000}{162,500}$$

$$= £1.20$$

14.2 D

	£
Actual expenditure	98,000
Less: Fixed cost over budget	11,000
Standard expenditure for 18,000 units	87,000
Less: Variable cost (18,000 × £2.75)	49,500
Budgeted fixed cost	37,500

14.3 C

Standard cost of direct labour	£1 per unit
17,600 units should have cost	£17,600
17,600 units did cost	£19,540
Direct labour variance is	£1,940 (A)

14.4 D

Variable overhead should have cost	£23,696

$$\left(\frac{£4,200}{20,000} \times 17,600\right)$$

Actual variable overhead	£3,660
Variable overhead variance	£36 (F)

14.5 A

£
5,400 (F)
2,400 (A)
3,000 (F)

14.6 A

Variable costs are conventionally deemed to be constant per unit of output.

14.7 C

A flexible budget is one which shows the costs and revenues at different levels of activity.

14.8 A

A criticism of fixed budgets is that they make no distinction between fixed and variable costs.

14.9 **C**

Production units	1,200	1,000
Cost	£9,800	£8,700
Difference per 200 units	£1,100	
Difference per 50 units	£275	

So £9,800 + 275 = £10,075.

14.10 **B**

The difference between the flexed budget and the actual results is known as the expenditure variance.

Mock Assessments

Mock Assessment 1

Certificate in Business Accounting
Fundamentals of Management Accounting

You are allowed two hours to complete this assessment.

The assessment contains 50 questions.

All questions are compulsory.

Do not turn the page until you are ready to attempt the assessment under timed conditions.

Mock Assessment Questions

Question 1
Which ONE of the following would be classified as direct labour?

- ☐ Personnel manager in a company servicing cars.
- ☐ Bricklayer in a construction company.
- ☐ General manager in a DIY shop.
- ☐ Maintenance manager in a company producing cameras.

Question 2
The principal budget factor is the

- ☐ factor which limits the activities of the organisation and is often the starting point in budget preparation.
- ☐ budgeted revenue expected in a forthcoming period.
- ☐ main budget into which all subsidiary budgets are consolidated.
- ☐ overestimation of revenue budgets and underestimation of cost budgets, which operates as a safety factor against risk.

Question 3
R Ltd absorbs overheads based on units produced. In one period 110,000 units were produced and the actual overheads were £500,000. Overheads were £50,000 over-absorbed in the period.

The overhead absorption rate was £☐ per unit.

Question 4
X Ltd operates an integrated cost accounting system. The Work-in-Progress Account at the end of the period showed the following information:

Work-in-Progress Account

	£		£
Stores ledger a/c	100,000	?	200,000
Wage control a/c	75,000		
Factory overhead a/c	50,000	Balance c/d	25,000
	225,000		225,000

The £200,000 credit entry represents the value of the transfer to the

- ☐ Cost of sales account.
- ☐ Material control account.
- ☐ Sales account.
- ☐ Finished goods inventory account.

Question 5

X Ltd absorbs overheads on the basis of machine hours. Details of budgeted and actual figures are as follows:

	Budget	Actual
Overheads	£1,250,000	£1,005,000
Machine hours	250,000 hours	220,000 hours

(a) Overheads for the period were:

under-absorbed ☐
over-absorbed ☐

(b) The value of the under/over absorption for the period was £_____.

Question 6

In an integrated bookkeeping system, when the actual production overheads exceed the absorbed production overheads, the accounting entries to close off the production overhead account at the end of the period would be:

	Debit	Credit	No entry in this account
Production overhead account	☐	☐	☐
Work in progress account	☐	☐	☐
Income statement	☐	☐	☐

Question 7

A retailer uses a Last In First Out (LIFO) inventory valuation system. Movements of item M for February are as follows.

	Units	£ per unit
1st February Opening inventory balance	230	7.80
3rd February Receipts	430	7.95
8th February Issues	370	
14th February Issues	110	
22nd February Receipts	400	8.01

No other movements of item M occurred during the month.

(a) The value of the closing inventory of item M at the end of February is £_____
(b) All units of item M were sold for £14 each. The gross profit achieved on item M during February was £_____

Question 8

A Limited has completed the initial allocation and apportionment of its overhead costs to cost centres as follows.

Cost centre	Initial allocation £000
Machining	190
Finishing	175
Stores	30
Maintenance	25
	420

The stores and maintenance costs must now be reapportioned taking account of the service they provide to each other as follows.

	Machining	Finishing	Stores	Maintenance
Stores to be apportioned	60%	30%	–	10%
Maintenance to be apportioned	75%	20%	5%	

After the apportionment of the service department costs, the total overhead cost of the production departments will be (*to the nearest £000*):

Machining £ ☐
Finishing £ ☐

Question 9

The budgeted contribution for R Limited last month was £32,000. The following variances were reported.

Variance	£	
Sales volume contribution	800	adverse
Material price	880	adverse
Material usage	822	favourable
Labour efficiency	129	favourable
Variable overhead efficiency	89	favourable

No other variances were reported for the month.
The actual contribution earned by R Limited last month was £ ☐

Question 10

The following scattergraph has been prepared for the costs incurred by an organisation that delivers hot meals to the elderly in their homes.

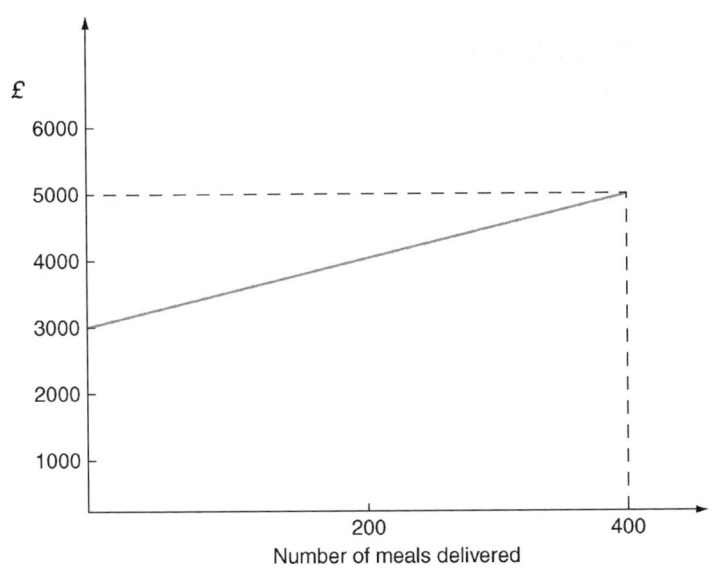

[Scattergraph: x-axis "Number of meals delivered" with markings at 200 and 400; y-axis "£" with markings at 1000, 2000, 3000, 4000, 5000, 6000. Line starts at £3000 at 0 meals and rises to £5000 at 400 meals.]

Based on the scattergraph:
(a) the period fixed cost is £ ☐
(b) the variable cost per meal delivered is £ ☐

Question 11

A company operates a differential piece-rate system and the following weekly rates have been set:

1–500 units	£0.20 per unit in this band
501–600 units	£0.25 per unit in this band
601 units and above	£0.55 per unit in this band

Details relating to employee A for the latest week are shown below:

Employee A
Actual output achieved   800 units
Actual hours worked   45

There is a guaranteed minimum wage of £5 per hour for a 40-hour week paid to all employees.

The amount payable (to the nearest £) to employee A is £ ☐.

Question 12

Overtime premium is

☐ the additional amount paid for hours worked in excess of the basic working week.
☐ the additional amount paid over and above the normal hourly rate for hours worked in excess of the basic working week.

☐ the additional amount paid over and above the overtime rate for hours worked in excess of the basic working week.
☐ the overtime rate.

Questions 13 and 14 are based on the following data

X Ltd has two production departments, Assembly and Finishing, and one service department, Stores.

Stores provide the following service to the production departments: 60% to Assembly and 40% to Finishing.

The budgeted information for the year is as follows:
Budgeted production overheads:

Assembly	£100,000
Finishing	£150,000
Stores	£50,000
Budgeted output	100,000 units

Question 13

The budgeted production overhead absorption rate for the Assembly Department will be £☐ per unit.

Question 14

At the end of the year, the total of all of the production overheads debited to the Finishing Department Production Overhead Control Account was £130,000, and the actual output achieved was 100,000 units.

(a) The overheads for the Finishing Department were:

under-absorbed ☐
over-absorbed ☐

(b) The value of the under/over absorption was £☐.

Question 15

R Ltd has been asked to quote for a job. The company aims to make a profit margin of 20% on sales. The estimated total variable production cost for the job is £125.

Fixed production overheads for the company are budgeted to be £250,000 and are recovered on the basis of labour hours. There are 12,500 budgeted labour hours and this job is expected to take 3 labour hours.

Other costs in relation to selling, distribution and administration are recovered at the rate of £15 per job.

The company quote for the job should be £☐.

Question 16

Which of the following would NOT be included in a cash budget? Tick all that would NOT be included.

- ☐ Depreciation
- ☐ Provisions for doubtful debts
- ☐ Wages and salaries

The following information is required for Questions 17 and 18

X Ltd is preparing its budgets for the forthcoming year.
The estimated sales for the first four months of the forthcoming year are as follows:

Month 1	6,000 units
Month 2	7,000 units
Month 3	5,500 units
Month 4	6,000 units

40% of each month's sales units are to be produced in the month of sale and the balance is to be produced in the previous month.

50% of the direct materials required for each month's production will be purchased in the previous month and the balance in the month of production.

The direct material cost is budgeted to be £5 per unit.

Question 17

The production budget for Month 1 will be ☐ units.

Question 18

The material cost budget for Month 2 will be £☐.

Question 19

When calculating the material purchases budget, the quantity to be purchased equals

- ☐ material usage + materials closing inventory − materials opening inventory
- ☐ material usage − materials closing inventory + materials opening inventory
- ☐ material usage − materials closing inventory − materials opening inventory
- ☐ material usage + materials closing inventory + materials opening inventory

Question 20

The following extract is taken from the overhead budget of X Ltd:

Budgeted activity	50%	75%
Budgeted overhead	£100,000	£112,500

The overhead budget for an activity level of 80% would be £☐.

168 Exam Practice Kit: Fundamentals of Management Accounting

Question 21

Which of the following would be included in the cash budget, but would not be included in the budgeted income statement? Tick all that are correct.

☐ Repayment of a bank loan.
☐ Proceeds from the sale of a non-current asset.
☐ Bad debts write off.

income statement

Question 22

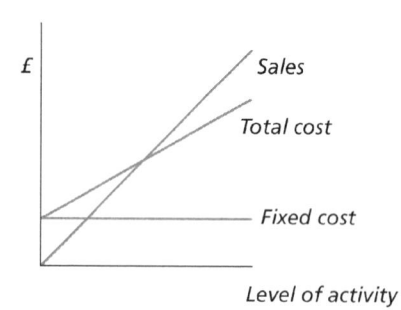

This graph is known as a

☐ semi-variable cost chart.
☐ conventional breakeven chart.
☐ contribution breakeven chart.
☐ profit volume chart.

Question 23

The following details have been extracted from the payables records of X Limited:

Invoices paid in the month of purchase	25%
Invoices paid in the first month after purchase	70%
Invoices paid in the second month after purchase	5%

Purchases for July to September are budgeted as follows:

July	£250,000
August	£300,000
September	£280,000

For suppliers paid in the month of purchase, a settlement discount of 5% is received. The amount budgeted to be paid to suppliers in September is £☐.

Question 24

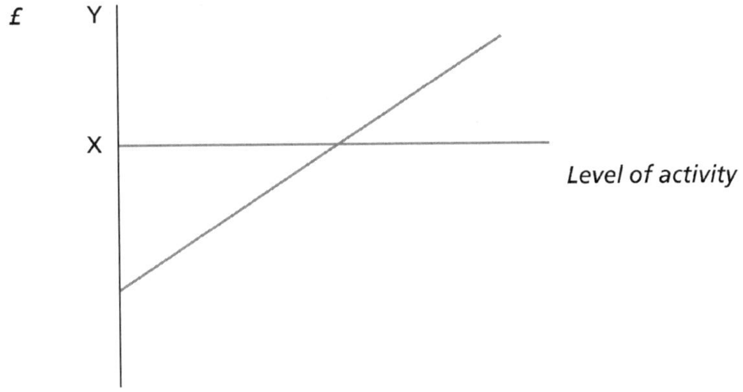
£
Y
X
Level of activity

The difference in the values (£) between point X and point Y on the profit volume chart shown above represents:

- ☐ contribution
- ☐ profit
- ☐ breakeven
- ☐ loss

Question 25

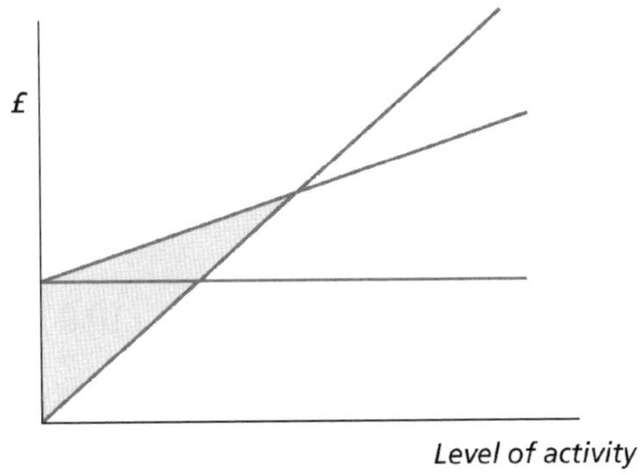
£
Level of activity

The shaded area on the breakeven chart shown above represents:

- ☐ loss
- ☐ fixed cost
- ☐ variable cost
- ☐ profit

Question 26

In a standard cost bookkeeping system, when the actual material usage has been greater than the standard material usage, the entries to record this in the accounts are:

	Debit	Credit	No entry in this account
Material usage variance account	☐	☐	☐
Raw material control account	☐	☐	☐
Work in progress account	☐	☐	☐

Question 27

R Ltd makes one product, which passes through a single process.
Details of the process for period 1 were as follows:

	£
Material cost – 20,000 kg	26,000
Labour cost	12,000
Production overhead cost	5,700
Output	18,800 kg
Normal losses	5% of input

There was no work-in-progress at the beginning or end of the period. Process losses have no value.

The cost of the abnormal loss (to the nearest £) is £ ☐.

Questions 28–35 are based on the following data

X Ltd operates a standard costing system. The following budgeted and standard cost information is available:

Budgeted production and sales	10,000 units
	£ per unit
Selling price	250
Direct material cost – 3 kg × £10	30
Direct labour cost – 5 hours × £8	40
Variable production overheads – 5 hours × £4	20

Actual results for the period were as follows:

Production and sales	11,500 units
	£
Sales value	2,817,500
Direct material – 36,000 kg	342,000
Direct labour – 52,000 hours	468,000
Variable production overheads	195,000

For all calculated variances, tick the correct box to indicate whether the variance is adverse or favourable.

Question 28

The direct material price variance is £☐

    adverse ☐
    favourable ☐

Question 29

The direct material usage variance is £☐

    adverse ☐
    favourable ☐

Question 30

The direct labour rate variance is £☐

    adverse ☐
    favourable ☐

Question 31

The direct labour efficiency variance is £☐

    adverse ☐
    favourable ☐

Question 32

The variable production overhead expenditure variance is £☐

    adverse ☐
    favourable ☐

Question 33

The variable production overhead efficiency variance is £☐

    adverse ☐
    favourable ☐

Question 34

The sales volume contribution variance is £☐

    adverse ☐
    favourable ☐

Question 35
The sales price variance is £☐☐☐☐

    adverse ☐
    favourable ☐

Question 36
X Ltd uses the FIFO method to charge material issue costs to production. Opening inventory of material M at the beginning of April was 270 units valued at £4 per unit.

Movements of material M during April was as follows.

    4 April   Received 30 units at £4.10 per unit
    9 April   Issued 210 units
    14 April   Issued 80 units
    22 April   Received 90 units at £4.20 per unit
    24 April   Issued 40 units

(a) The total value of the issues to production during April was £☐☐☐☐.
(b) The value of the closing inventory at the end of April was £☐☐☐☐.

Question 37
X Ltd manufactures a product called the 'ZT'. The budget for next year was:

Annual sales	10,000 units
	£ per unit
Selling price	20
Variable cost	14
Fixed costs	3
Profit	3

If the selling price of the ZT were reduced by 10 per cent, the sales revenue that would be needed to generate the original budgeted profit would be £☐☐☐☐.

Question 38
A company is faced with a shortage of skilled labour next period.

When determining the production plan that will maximise the company's profit next period, the company's products should be ranked according to their:

☐ profit per hour of skilled labour
☐ profit per unit of product sold
☐ contribution per hour of skilled labour
☐ contribution per unit of product sold

Question 39

Which of the following would contribute towards a favourable sales price variance (tick all that apply)?

(a) The standard sales price per unit was set too high ☐.
(b) Price competition in the market was not as fierce as expected ☐.
(c) Sales volume was higher than budgeted and therefore sales revenue was higher than budgeted ☐.

Question 40

R Ltd has the following year-end information regarding one of its long-term contracts:

	£
Revenue credited to income statement	2,500,000
Profit recognised	750,000
Cash received	1,875,000
Costs to date	2,200,000
Future costs	220,000

(a) The cost charged to the income statement in respect of this contract was £ ☐.
(b) The value of the contract account receivable is £ ☐.

Question 41

The following data relate to a process for the latest period.

Opening work in progress	300 kg valued as follows
	Input material £1,000
	Conversion cost £200
Input during period	8,000 kg at a cost of £29,475
Conversion costs	£11,977
Output	7,000 kg
Closing work in progress	400 kg

Closing work in progress is complete as to input materials and 70 per cent complete as to conversion costs.

Losses are expected to be 10 per cent of input during the period and they occur at the end of the process. Losses have a scrap value of £2 per kg.

The value of the completed output (to the nearest £) is £ ☐

Question 42

Which of the following inventory valuation methods results in charges to cost of sales which are close to the economic cost?

First In, First Out (FIFO) ☐
Last In, First Out (LIFO) ☐
Average Cost (AVCO) ☐

Questions 43 and 44 are based on the following data

A company makes a single product T and budgets to produce and sell 7,200 units each period. Cost and revenue data for the product at this level of activity are as follows.

	$ per unit
Selling price	53
Direct material cost	24
Direct labour cost	8
Other variable cost	3
Fixed cost	7
Profit	11

Question 43

The contribution to sales ratio (P/V ratio) of product T (to the nearest whole number) is ☐ %.

Question 44

The margin of safety of product T (to the nearest whole number) is ☐ % of budgeted sales volume.

Questions 45 and 46 are based on the following data

The total figures from TY Division's budgetary control report are as follows.

	Fixed budget $	Flexed budget allowances $	Actual results $
Total sales revenue	520,000	447,000	466,500
Total variable cost	389,000	348,000	329,400
Total contribution	131,000	99,000	137,100

Question 45

(a) The sales price variance for the period is $☐ **adverse/favourable**
(b) The sales volume contribution variance for the period is $☐ **adverse/favourable**

Question 46

(a) The total expenditure variance for the period is $☐ **adverse/favourable**
(b) The total budget variance for the period is $☐ **adverse/favourable**

Question 47

In an integrated bookkeeping system, the correct entries to record the depreciation of production machinery are:

	Debit	Credit	No entry in this account
Depreciation of production machinery	☐	☐	☐
Work in progress account	☐	☐	☐
Production overhead control account	☐	☐	☐

Question 48

In an integrated bookkeeping system, the correct entries to record the issue of indirect materials for production purposes are:

	Debit	Credit	No entry in this account
Materials control account	☐	☐	☐
Work in progress account	☐	☐	☐
Production overhead control account	☐	☐	☐

Question 49

H Limited budgets to produce and sell 4,000 units of product H next year. The amount of capital investment required to support product H will be £290,000 and H Limited requires a rate of return of 14 per cent on all capital invested.

The full cost per unit of product H is £45.90.

To the nearest penny, the selling price per unit of product H that will achieve the specified return on investment is £☐.

Question 50

The Drop In Café sells specialist coffees to customers to drink on the premises or to take away.

The proprietors have established that the cost of ingredients is a wholly variable cost in relation to the number of cups of coffee sold whereas staff costs are semi-variable and rent costs are fixed.

Within the relevant range, as the number of cups of coffee sold increases (delete as appropriate):

(a) The ingredients cost per cup sold will increase/decrease/stay the same.
(b) The staff cost per cup sold will increase/decrease/stay the same.
(c) The rent cost per cup sold will increase/decrease/stay the same.

First Mock Assessment – Solutions

✓ Solution 1

Bricklayer in a construction company.

The bricklayer's wages can be identified with a specific cost unit therefore this is a direct cost. The wages paid to the other three people cannot be identified with specific cost units. Therefore they would be indirect costs.

✓ Solution 2

The principal budget factor is the factor which limits the activities of the organisation and is often the starting point in budget preparation.

✓ Solution 3

The overhead absorption rate was £5 per unit.

Workings:

	£
Actual overheads	500,000
Over absorption	50,000
Overhead absorbed	550,000

Overhead absorption rate = £550,000/110,000 units = £5.

✓ Solution 4

Finished goods inventory account.

✓ Solution 5

Overheads for the period were *over-absorbed by £95,000*.

Workings:
Overhead absorption rate = £1,250,000/250,000 = £5 per hour

	£
Absorbed overhead = 220,000 hours × £5	1,100,000
Actual overhead incurred	1,005,000
Over-absorbed overhead	95,000

✓ Solution 6

	Debit	Credit	No entry in this account
Income statement			
Production overhead account		✓	
Work in progress account			✓
Income statement	✓		

Solution 7

(a) The value of the closing inventory of item M at the end of February is £4,608
(b) All units of item M were sold for £14 each. The gross profit achieved on item M during February was £2,911.50

Workings

		Receipts			Sales			Balance	
Date	Qty	Price	£	Qty	Price	£	Qty	Price	£
1 Feb							230	7.80	1,794.00
3 Feb	430	7.95	3,418.50				230	7.80	1,794.00
							430	7.95	3,418.50
							660		5,212.50
8 Feb				370	7.95	2,941.50	230	7.80	1,794.00
							60	7.95	477.00
							290		2,271.00
14 Feb				60	7.95	477.00			
				50	7.80	390.00			
				110		867.00	180	7.80	1,404.00
22 Feb	400	8.01	3,204.00				180	7.80	1,404.00
							400	8.01	3,204.00
							580		4,608.00

(b)

	£
Sales revenue (480 units × £14)	6,720.00
Cost of goods sold (2,941.50 + 867.00)	3,808.50
Gross profit	2,911.50

Solution 8

After the apportionment of the service department costs, the total overhead cost of the production departments will be (*to the nearest £000*):

Machining £230,000
Finishing £190,000

Workings

	Machining	Finishing	Stores	Maintenance
	£000	£000	£000	£000
Apportioned costs	190.00	175.00	30.0	25.0
Stores apportionment	18.00	9.00	(30.0)	3.0
Maintenance apportionment	21.00	5.60	1.4	(28.0)
Stores apportionment	0.84	0.42	(1.4)	0.14
Maintenance apportionment	0.11	0.03	–	(0.14)
Total	229.95	190.05		

Solution 9

The actual contribution earned by R Limited last month was £31,360.

£(32,000 − 800 − 880 + 822 + 129 + 89) = £31,360.

Solution 10

(a) The period fixed cost is £3,000
(b) The variable cost per meal delivered is £5

Workings:

$$\text{Variable cost per meal} = \frac{£5,000 - £3,000}{400 \text{ meals}} = £5$$

Solution 11

The amount payable to employee A is £235.

Workings:

Units		£
500 × 20p		100
100 × 25p		25
200 × 55p		110
800		235

Solution 12

Overtime premium is the additional amount paid over and above the normal hourly rate for hours worked in excess of the basic working week.

Solution 13

The budgeted production overhead absorption rate for the Assembly Department will be £1.30 per unit.

Workings:

	Assembly £
Budgeted overheads	100,000
Reapportioned stores overhead 60% × £50,000	30,000
Total budgeted overhead	130,000
Budgeted output	100,000
OAR =	£130,000 / 100,000 = £1.30 per unit

Solution 14

The overheads for the Finishing Department were *over-absorbed by £40,000*.

Workings:

	Finishing
	£
Budgeted overheads	150,000
Reapportioned stores overhead 40% × £50,000	20,000
Total budgeted overhead	170,000
Budgeted output	100,000

$$\text{OAR} = \frac{£170,000}{100,000} = £1.70 \text{ per unit}$$

	£
Absorbed overhead £1.70 × 100,000	170,000
Actual overhead incurred	130,000
Over absorption	40,000

Solution 15

The company quote for the job should be *£250*.

Workings:

	Job quote
	£
Variable production costs	125
Fixed production overheads $\left(\frac{£250,000}{12,500} \times 3\right)$	60
Selling, distribution and administration	15
Total cost	200
Profit margin 20%	50
Quote	250

Solution 16

Depreciation and provisions for doubtful debts are not cash flows and would not be included in a cash budget.

✅ Solution 17

The production budget for month 1 will be *6,600 units*.

Workings:

	Month 1 Units	Month 2 Units	Month 3 Units	Month 4 Units
Sales	6,000	7,000	5,500	6,000
Production				
40% in the month	2,400	2,800	2,200	2,400
60% in the previous month	4,200	3,300	3,600	
Production	6,600	6,100	5,800	

✅ Solution 18

The material cost budget for Month 2 will be £30,500.

Workings:

Month 2   6,100 units produced @ £5 per unit = £30,500.

✅ Solution 19

The quantity to be purchased equals material usage + materials closing inventory − materials opening inventory

✅ Solution 20

The overhead budget for an activity level of 80% would be £115,000.

Workings:
Using the high/low method

		£	
High	75%	112,500	
Low	50%	100,000	
Change	25%	12,500	– variable cost of 25%
	1%	500	– variable cost of 1%

	£
Substitute into 75% activity	
Total overhead	112,500
Variable cost element 75 × £500	37,500
Fixed cost element	75,000
Total overhead for 80% activity	
Variable cost element 80 × £500	40,000
Fixed cost element	75,000
Total overhead	115,000

Solution 21

The correct answers are:
- repayment of a bank loan
- proceeds from the sale of a non-current asset.

Both these items result in a cash flow and would therefore be included in the cash budget. However, they would not be included in the income statement. The bad debts write off would be included in the income statement, but not in the cash budget.

Solution 22

The graph is known as a conventional breakeven chart.

Solution 23

The amount budgeted to be paid to suppliers in September is £289,000.

Workings:

	July £	August £	September £
Purchases	250,000	300,000	280,000
25% paid in the month of purchase	62,500	75,000	70,000
5% discount allowed	(3,125)	(3,750)	(3,500)
70% paid in the first month		175,000	210,000
5% paid in the second month			12,500
Budgeted payment			289,000

Solution 24

The difference in the values (£) between point X and point Y on the profit volume chart represents *profit*.

Solution 25

The shaded area on the breakeven chart represents *loss*.

Solution 26

	Debit	Credit	No entry in this account
Material usage variance account	✔		
Raw material control account			✔
Work in progress account		✔	

Solution 27

The cost of the abnormal loss is £460.

Workings:

	£
Direct material cost	26,000
Labour cost	12,000
Production overhead cost	5,700
	43,700

	Kg
Input	20,000
Normal loss	1,000
Expected output	19,000
Actual output	18,800
Abnormal loss	200

Cost per kg = £43,700/19,000 = £2.30
Cost of abnormal loss = £2.30 × 200 kg = £460.

Solution 28

The direct material price variance is £18,000 *favourable*.

Workings:

	£
36,000 kg should cost (× £10)	360,000
but did cost	342,000
Variance	18,000 F

Solution 29

The direct material usage variance is £15,000 *adverse*.

Workings:

11,500 units should use (× 3 kg)	34,500 kg
but did use	36,000 kg
Difference	1,500 kg
× std price per kg	× £10
Variance	£15,000 A

Solution 30

The direct labour rate variance is £52,000 *adverse*.

Workings:

	£
52,000 hours should cost (× £8)	416,000
but did cost	468,000
Variance	52,000 A

Solution 31

The direct labour efficiency variance is £44,000 *favourable*.

Workings:

11,500 units should take (× 5 hours)	57,500 hours
but did take	52,000 hours
Difference	5,500 hours
× std rate per hour	× £8
Variance	£44,000 F

Solution 32

The variable production overhead expenditure variance is £13,000 *favourable*.

Workings:

	£
52,000 hours should have cost (× £4)	208,000
but did cost	195,000
Variance	13,000 F

Solution 33

The variable production overhead efficiency variance is £22,000 *favourable*.

Workings:

Variance in hours from labour efficiency variance	= 5,500 hours
× standard variable production overhead per hour	× £4
Variance	£22,000 F

Solution 34

The sales volume contribution variance is £240,000 *favourable*.

Workings:

Actual sales volume	11,500	units
Budget sales volume	10,000	units
Variance in units	1,500	favourable
× standard contribution per unit £(250 − 30 − 40 − 20)	× £160	
Sales volume contribution variance	£240,000	favourable

Solution 35

The sales price variance is £57,500 *adverse*.

Workings:

	£
11,500 units should sell for (× £250)	2,875,000
But did sell for	2,817,500
Sales price variance	57,500 adverse

Solution 36

(a) The total value of the issues to production during April was *£1,329*.
(b) The value of the closing inventory at the end of April was *£252*.

Workings:

(a) Issues:

			£
9 April	210 units × £4		840
14 April	60 units × £4		240
	20 units × £4.10		82
24 April	10 units × £4.10		41
	30 units × £4.20		126
			1,329

(b) Inventory = 60 units × £4.20 = £252

Solution 37

The sales revenue that would be needed to generate the original budgeted profit would be £270,000.

Workings:
Fixed costs are not relevant because they will remain unaltered.
Original budgeted contribution = 10,000 units × £(20 − 14) = £60,000
Revised contribution per unit = £(18 − 14) = £4
Required number of units to achieve same contribution = £60,000/£4 = 15,000 units
Required sales revenue = 15,000 units × £18 revised price = £270,000

Solution 38

When determining the production plan that will maximise the company's profit next period, the company's products should be ranked according to their contribution per hour of skilled labour.

Solution 39

Only reason (b) would contribute to a favourable sales price variance.

Reason (a) would result in an adverse variance. Reason (c) would not necessarily result in any sales price variance because all the units could have been sold at standard price.

Solution 40

(a) The cost charged to the income statement in respect of this contract was £1,750,000.

Workings:

	£
Revenue credited	2,500,000
Profit recognised	750,000
Cost charged	1,750,000

(b) The value of the contract account receivable is £625,000.

Workings:

	£
Revenue credited	2,500,000
Less cash received	1,875,000
Debtor balance	625,000

Solution 41

The value of the completed output is £38,500

Workings

					Equivalent kg	
				Input material		Conversion costs
Input	kg	Output	kg			
Opening WIP	300	Finished output	7,000	7,000		7,000
Input	8,000	Normal loss	800	–		–
		Abnormal loss	100	100		100
		Closing WIP	400	400	70%	280
	8,300		8,300	7,500		7,380

	£	£		£
Costs				
Opening WIP	1,200	1,000		200
Period costs	41,452	29,475		11,977
Normal loss	(1,600)	(1,600)		–
	41,052	28,875		12,177
Cost per equivalent kg	5.50	3.85		1.65

The value of the completed output is £5.50 × 7,000 kg = £38,500

Solution 42

The LIFO inventory valuation method results in charges to cost of sales which are close to the economic cost.

Solution 43

The contribution to sales ratio (P/V ratio) of product T is 34%.

Workings:
Contribution per unit of product T = $(53 − 24 − 8 − 3) = $18
Contribution to sales ratio = 18/53 = 34%

Solution 44

The margin of safety of product T is 61% of budgeted sales volume.

Workings:
Period fixed costs = 7,200 × $7 = $50,400

$$\text{Breakeven point} = \frac{\$50,400}{\$18} = 2,800 \text{ units}$$

Margin of safety = (7,200 − 2,800) units = 4,400 units
Margin of safety as percentage of budgeted sales = 4,400/7,200 = 61%

Solution 45

(a) The sales price variance is $(466,500 − 447,000) = $19,500 favourable
(b) The sales volume contribution variance is $(99,000 − 131,000) = $32,000 adverse

Solution 46

(a) The total expenditure variance is $(329,400 − 348,000) = $18,600 favourable
(b) The total budget variance is $(137,100 − 131,000) = $6,100 favourable

Solution 47

	Debit	Credit	No entry in this account
Depreciation of production machinery		✔	
Work in progress account			✔
Production overhead control account	✔		

Solution 48

	Debit	Credit	No entry in this account
Materials control account		✓	
Work in progress account			✓
Production overhead control account	✓		

Solution 49

The selling price per unit of product H that will achieve the specified return on investment is £56.05

Workings:
Required return from capital invested to support product H = £290,000 × 14%
= £40,600

Required return per unit of product H sold = £40,600/4,000 = £10.15
Required selling price = £45.90 full cost + £10.15 = £56.05

Solution 50

Within the relevant range, as the number of cups of coffee sold increases:

(a) the ingredients cost per cup sold will stay the same.
(b) the staff cost per cup sold will decrease.
(c) the rent cost per cup sold will decrease.

Mock Assessment 2

Certificate in Business Accounting
Fundamentals of Management Accounting

You are allowed two hours to complete this assessment.

The assessment contains 50 questions.

All questions are compulsory.

Do not turn the page until you are ready to attempt the assessment under timed conditions.

Mock Assessment Questions

Question 1

The total cost of direct materials, direct labour and direct expenses is known as:

(A) A cost unit
(B) A direct cost
(C) A prime cost
(D) An indirect cost

Question 2

Which of the following are examples of semi-fixed costs?

(i) Raw materials
(ii) Telephone
(iii) Electricity
(iv) Rent

(A) (i) and (ii)
(B) (ii) and (iii)
(C) (i) and (iv)
(D) (ii) and (iv)

Question 3

Using the high–low method, the fixed and variable elements of cost for September based on the following information were:

	Units	Cost
July	400	£1,000
August	500	£1,200
September	600	£1,400
October	700	£1,600
November	800	£1,800
December	900	£2,000

(A) Fixed cost £200 – Variable cost £200
(B) Fixed cost £1,000 – Variable cost £400
(C) Fixed cost £200 – Variable cost £1,200
(D) Fixed cost £400 – Variable cost £1,000

Question 4

The main advantage of using a FIFO system of inventory valuation is that:

(A) It produces realistic inventory valuations
(B) It produces up-to-date production costs
(C) It simplifies inventory records
(D) None of the above

Question 5

A company purchases and resells a single item of a product. Opening inventory on 1st January was 200 units valued at £1.80. During the month, the following transactions were recorded:

	Units	£ per unit
Receipts		
7th January	300	£2.10
15th January	250	–
Sales		
25th January	625	£4.00

The company uses the FIFO method of inventory valuation, gross profit for the month was £1,250. The cost of the 250 units received on 15th January was:

(A) £2.00
(B) £2.08
(C) £2.25
(D) £2.35

Question 6

The following information is available concerning Material X for May.

	Units	£ per unit
Opening inventory	100	£70.00
Receipts		
9 May	150	£71.70
22 May	100	£72.20
Issues to production		
4 May	80	
15 May	120	

The company uses the weighted average method of inventory valuation.

The price per unit of the issues to production on 15 May was £_____

Questions 7 and 8 are based on the following data

Receipts and issues of PART SKI for the month of March are as follows:

	Receipts Units	Value (£)	Issues units
3rd March	2,000	12,000	
7th March	3,000	19,800	
11th March	2,000	16,000	
16th March			4,000
24th March	3,000	21,000	
30th March			5,000

Opening inventory of SKI was 1,000 units valued at £5.60 each.

Question 7

Using the FIFO method of inventory valuation, the cost of the issued parts in March was:

(A) £60,400
(B) £61,800
(C) £62,800
(D) £66,000

Question 8

Using the LIFO method of inventory valuation, the cost of the issued parts in March was:

(A) £60,400
(B) £61,800
(C) £62,800
(D) £66,000

Question 9

The process of cost apportionment is carried out so that:

(A) costs may be controlled
(B) cost units gather overheads as they pass through cost centres
(C) whole items of cost can be charged to cost centres
(D) common costs are shared among cost centres

Questions 10 and 11 are based on the following data

Budgeted labour hours	8,500
Budgeted overheads	£148,750
Actual labour hours	7,928
Actual overheads	£146,200

Question 10

The labour hour overhead absorption rate for the period was:

(A) £17.20 per hour
(B) £17.50 per hour
(C) £18.44 per hour
(D) £18.76 per hour

Question 11

Overheads during the period were:

(A) Under-absorbed by £2,550
(B) Over-absorbed by £2,529
(C) Over-absorbed by £2,550
(D) Under-absorbed by £7,460

Question 12

A company absorbs overheads based on machine hours which are budgeted at 11,250 hours at £23 per hour. If actual machine hours worked were 10,980 hours and overheads were £254,692 then overheads were:

(A) Under-absorbed by £2,152
(B) Over-absorbed by £4,058
(C) Under-absorbed by £4,058
(D) Over-absorbed by £2,152

Question 13

Is the following statement true or false?

Overheads will always be under-absorbed when actual overhead expenditure is higher than budgeted for the period.

Question 14

After the initial overhead allocation and apportionment has been completed, the overhead analysis sheet for a factory is as follows.

Overhead cost	Machining	Finishing & packing	Stores	Maintenance
£57,440	£24,100	£17,930	£5,070	£10,340

The costs of maintenance are to be reapportioned to the other three cost centres according to the number of maintenance hours worked, which are as follows.

	Machining	Finishing & packing	Stores	Maintenance
Maintenance hours	3,800	850	50	100

The maintenance cost (to the nearest £) to be apportioned to the machining department is £_____

Question 15

A cost centre absorbs production overhead on the basis of machine hours. Last period the overhead was under-absorbed by £20,000. The actual production overhead incurred was £280,000 and 40,000 machine hours were worked.

The overhead absorption rate per machine hour was £_____

Question 16

A company manufactures a range of products, including product G for which the total cost is £32 per unit. The company's budgeted total cost for the period is £580,000 and the budgeted rate of return on the capital employed of £435,000 is 20%.

The cost-plus selling price of one unit of product G should be (to the nearest penny) £_____

Question 17

Which of the following can be used as a measure of pre-determined overhead rates in absorption costing?

(i) Number of units
(ii) Number of labour hours
(iii) Number of machine hours

(A) (i) and (ii)
(B) (ii) and (iii)
(C) (i) and (iii)
(D) (i), (ii) and (iii)

❓ Question 18

Which of the following best describes contribution?

(A) Profit
(B) Sales value less variable cost of sales
(C) Sales value plus variable cost
(D) Fixed cost less variable cost

Questions 19 to 22 are based on the following data

Sales (units)   1,000
Selling price   £10
Variable cost   £6
Fixed costs   £2,500

❓ Question 19

The contribution/sales ratio is:

(A) 20%
(B) 37.5%
(C) 40%
(D) 60%

❓ Question 20

The number of units sold in order to break-even is:

(A) 100 units
(B) 375 units
(C) 625 units
(D) 1,000 units

❓ Question 21

The margin of safety is:

(A) 10%
(B) 37.5%
(C) 40%
(D) 50%

❓ Question 22

How much revenue would we need to generate to produce a profit of £5,000?

(A) £10,000
(B) £12,250
(C) £18,750
(D) £23,000

Question 23

If selling price is £100 and unit cost is £40, then:

(A) Gross profit margin is 60% and mark-up is 150%
(B) Gross profit margin is 150% and mark-up is 60%
(C) Gross profit margin and mark-up are the same
(D) Not enough information given to calculate these figures

Question 24

Which of the following statements is correct?

(A) The point where the total cost line cuts the vertical axis is the breakeven point on a traditional breakeven chart
(B) The point where the total cost line cuts the horizontal axis is the breakeven point on a traditional breakeven chart
(C) The point where the profit line cuts the horizontal axis is the breakeven point on a profit-volume chart
(D) The point where the profit line cuts the vertical axis is the breakeven point on a profit-volume chart

Question 25

Product R sells for £45 per unit and incurs variable cost of £15 per unit and fixed cost of £30,000.

The line drawn on a profit-volume chart will cut the vertical (y) axis at the point where $y =$ _____

Question 26

A company makes and sells three products for which information is as follows.

	Product E £ per unit	Product F £ per unit	Product G £ per unit
Direct labour (£15 per hour)	7.50	22.50	15.00
Direct material (£8 per kg)	12.00	10.00	16.00
Maximum demand per period (units)	380	520	240

Labour hours are limited to 1,300 hours each period and the supply of material is limited to 1,450 kg each period.

What is the company's limiting factor(s)?

(A) Direct labour
(B) Direct material
(C) Both direct material and direct labour
(D) Neither direct material nor direct labour

Question 27

Simpkins Ltd is currently experiencing a shortage of skilled labour. In the coming quarter only 3,600 hours will be available for the production of the firm's three products for which details are shown below:

Product	X	Y	Z
Selling price per unit	£66	£100	£120
Variable cost per unit	£42	£75	£90
Fixed cost per unit	£30	£34	£40
Skilled labour per unit	0.40 hours	0.50 hours	0.75 hours
Maximum quarterly demand	5,000	5,000	2,000

The optimum production plan that will maximise profit for the quarter is:

(A)   0 X's   2,200 Y's   and   2,000 Z's
(B)   5,000 X's   200 Y's   and   2,000 Z's
(C)   5,000 X's   3,200 Y's   and   0 Z's
(D)   9,000 X's   0 Y's   and   0 Z's

Question 28

A standard based on last period's actuals or the average of some previous period is known as:

(A) A basic standard
(B) An ideal standard
(C) An attainable standard
(D) An historical standard

Questions 29 and 30 are based on the following information

In week 50 a factory had an activity level of 120%:

	Units	Standard minutes each
Product A	5,100	6
Product B	2,520	10
Product C	3,150	12

The budgeted direct labour cost for budgeted output was £2,080.

Question 29

The budgeted standard hours were:

(A) 2,080
(B) 1,560
(C) 1,300
(D) 1,100

Question 30

The budgeted labour cost per standard hour was:

(A) £1
(B) £1.20
(C) £1.60
(D) £2

Questions 31 and 32 are based on the following data

PP Ltd has prepared the following standard cost information for one unit of product X:

Direct materials	2 kg at £13/per kg	£26.00
Direct labour	3.3 hours at £4/per hour	£13.20

Actual results for the period were recorded as follows:

Production	12,000 units
Materials – 26,400 kg	£336,600
Labour – 40,200 hours	£168,840

All of the materials were purchased and used during the period.

Question 31

The direct material price and usage variances are:

	Material price	Material usage
A	£6,600 (F)	£31,200 (A)
B	£6,600 (F)	£31,200 (F)
C	£31,200 (F)	£6,600 (A)
D	£31,200 (A)	£6,600 (A)

Question 32

The direct labour rate and efficiency variances are:

	Labour rate	Labour efficiency
A	£8,040 (A)	£2,400 (A)
B	£8,040 (A)	£2,400 (F)
C	£8,040 (F)	£2,400 (A)
D	£8,040 (F)	£2,400 (F)

Questions 33 and 34 are based on the following information

The standard selling price of product Y is £34 per unit and the standard variable cost is £20 per unit. Budgeted sales volume is 45,000 units each period.

Last period a total of 46,000 units were sold and the revenue achieved was £1,495,000.

Question 33

The sales price variance for the period was £_____

Question 34

The sales volume contribution variance for the period was £_____

Question 35

In an integrated cost and financial accounting system, the accounting entries for production overhead absorbed would be:

A   DR – WIP control account
      CR – overhead control account
B   DR – overhead control account
      CR – WIP account
C   DR – overhead control account
      CR – cost of sales account
D   DR – cost of sales account
      CR – WIP control account

Questions 36 – 39 are based on the following data

X plc makes one product, which passes through a single process.

Details of the process are as follows:

Materials: 5,000 kg at 50p per kg
Labour: £800
Production overheads 200% of labour

Normal losses are 20 per cent of input in the process, and without further processing any losses can be sold as scrap for 30p per kg.

The output for the period was 3,800 kg from the process.

There was no work-in-progress at the beginning or end of the period.

? Question 36

What value will be credited to the process account for the scrap value of the normal loss?

(A) £300
(B) £530
(C) £980
(D) £1,021

? Question 37

What is the value of the abnormal loss?

(A) £60
(B) £196
(C) £230
(D) £245

? Question 38

What is the value of the output?

(A) £3,724
(B) £4,370
(C) £4,655
(D) £4,900

Questions 39 to 41 are based on the following data

A product is manufactured as a result of two processes, A and B. Details of process B for the month of August were as follows:

Materials transferred from process A	10,000 kg valued at £40,500
Labour costs	1,000 hours @ £5.616 per hour
Overheads	50% of labour costs
Output transferred to finished goods	8,000 kg
Closing work-in-progress	900 kg

Normal loss is 10 per cent of input and losses do not have a scrap value.

Closing work-in-progress is 100 per cent complete for material, and 75 per cent complete for both labour and overheads.

Question 39

What is the value of the abnormal loss (to the nearest £)?

(A) Nil
(B) £489
(C) £544
(D) £546

Question 40

What is the value of the output (to the nearest £)?

(A) £39,139
(B) £43,488
(C) £43,680
(D) £43,977

Question 41

What is the value of the closing work-in-progress (to the nearest £)?

(A) £4,403
(B) £4,698
(C) £4,892
(D) £4,947

Question 42

Which of the following items would appear on a job cost sheet?

(i) materials purchased specifically for the job
(ii) materials drawn from inventory
(iii) direct wages
(iv) direct expenses

(A) (i) and (ii)
(B) (iii) and (iv)
(C) (i), (ii) and (iii)
(D) (i), (ii), (iii) and (iv)

Question 43

A retailer buys in a product for £50 per unit and wishes to achieve 40% gross profit on sales. The selling price is:

(A) £70
(B) £83.33
(C) £90
(D) £125

Questions 44 and 45 are based on the following data

A small management consultancy has prepared the following information:

Overhead absorption rate per consulting hour	£12.50
Salary cost per consulting hour (senior)	£20.00
Salary cost per consulting hour (junior)	£15.00

The firm adds 40% to total cost to arrive at a selling price.

Assignment number 652 took 86 hours of a senior consultant's time and 220 hours of a junior consultant's time.

Question 44

What price should be charged for assignment 652?

(A) £5,355
(B) £7,028
(C) £8,845
(D) £12,383

Question 45

During a period 3,000 consulting hours were charged out in the ratio of 1 senior to 3 junior hours. Overheads were exactly as budgeted.

What was the total gross profit for the period?

(A) £34,500
(B) £48,300
(C) £86,250
(D) £120,750

Question 46

The total estimated cost of job no. 387 is £2,080. The company requires a profit margin of 20 per cent of the selling price. The price to be quoted for job no.387 is £_____

Question 47

A construction company has the following data concerning one of its contracts:

Contract price	£2,000,000
Value certified	£1,300,000
Cash received	£1,200,000
Costs incurred	£1,050,000
Cost of work certified	£1,000,000

The profit (to the nearest £1,000) to be attributed to the contract is:

(A) £250,000
(B) £277,000
(C) £300,000
(D) £950,000

Question 48

A company budgets to sell the following number of units of product X.

	January	February	March
Sales units	500	560	590

Inventory of product X at the end of each month is budgeted to be 20 per cent of the number of units required for the following month's sales.

Budgeted production of product X during February is _____ units.

Question 49

The following extract is taken from the maintenance cost budget:

Maintenance hours	8,300	8,520
Maintenance cost	£211,600	£216,440

The budget cost allowance for maintenance costs for the latest period, when 8,427 maintenance hours were worked, is £_____

Question 50

A company makes 20 per cent of its sales for cash. The following information is available concerning the collection of amounts owing from the credit customers.

Invoices paid in the month after sale	70%
Invoices paid in the second month after sale	27%
Bad debts	3%

Credit customers who pay in the month after sale receive a 2% discount.

Budgeted sales revenues are as follows.

January	February	March
£75,800	£72,900	£66,200

The receipts from customers in March (to the nearest £) are budgeted to be £_____

Mock Assessment 2 – Solutions

✅ Solution 1

On an individual basis, materials, labour and direct expenses are direct costs but collectively, they are often known as prime costs.

So C.

✅ Solution 2

A semi-fixed cost such as telephone and electricity is part fixed and part variable. We pay a fixed cost to have access to these services and a variable cost based on usage.

So (ii) and (iii) - **Answer B.**

✅ Solution 3

Highest	900
Lowest	400
Difference	500 units
Difference in cost	£1,000

Variable cost per unit = £2. At 400 units – if variable cost is £2 per unit and total cost is £1,000, then variable cost must be £800, so fixed cost must be £200.

So for September, fixed cost is £200 – so variable cost must be 600 × £2 = £1,200.

So C.

✅ Solution 4

The main advantage of using FIFO is that it produces realistic inventory valuations since the price of the most recently purchased items is used.

So A.

✅ Solution 5

Sales – 625 ×£4	£2,500
Gross profit	£1,250
Material cost of sales	£1,250

Cost of units sold:

Opening inventory	200 × £1.80	£360
7th Jan	300 × £2.10	£630
		£990
Material cost of goods sold		£1,250
Therefore, 125 units (balance) cost		£260

So cost per unit is £260 / 125 = £2.08

So B.

✓ Solution 6

		Units	£ per unit	Total £
1 May	Opening inventory	100	£70.00	7,000
4 May	Issues	(80)	£70.00	(5,600)
		20	£70.00	1,400
9 May	Receipts	150	£71.70	10,755
		170		12,155

Price per unit of issues on 15 May = £12,155/170 = £71.50

✓ Solution 7

Opening inventory	£5.60 per unit
3rd	£6 per unit
7th	£6.60 per unit
11th	£8 per unit
24th	£7 per unit

Value of parts issued:

		£
16th	1,000 at £5.60	5,600
	2,000 at £6	12,000
	1,000 at £6.60	6,600
		24,200
30th	2,000 at £6.60	13,200
	2,000 at £8	16,000
	1,000 at £7	7,000
		36,200

£24,200 + £36,200 = £60,400

So A.

✓ Solution 8

Using LIFO:

		£
16th	2,000 at £8	16,000
	2,000 at £6.60	13,200
		29,200
30th	3,000 at £7	21,000
	1,000 at £6.60	6,600
	1,000 at £6	6,000
		33,600

Total value of parts issued £62,800

So C.

✅ Solution 9

The process of cost apportionment is carried out so that common costs are shared among cost centres.

So D.

✅ Solution 10

$$\frac{\text{Budgeted overheads}}{\text{Budgeted labour hours}} \quad \frac{£148{,}750}{8{,}500}$$

= £17.50 per hour.

So B.

✅ Solution 11

Actual hours × absorption rate

= 7,928 × £17.50 = £138,740

	£
Actual overhead	146,200
Amount absorbed	138,740
Under absorption	7,460

So D.

✅ Solution 12

Actual overheads	£254,692
Actual hours × absorption rate	
10,980 × £23	£252,540

Overheads were under-absorbed by £2,152.

So A.

✅ Solution 13

The statement is <u>false.</u>

If the actual activity level is also higher than budgeted then additional overhead will have been absorbed. It is possible for overhead to be over-absorbed in this situation.

✅ Solution 14

Maintenance cost per hour in the three cost centres = £10,340/(3,800 + 850 + 50) = £2.20

Cost to be apportioned to machining department = £2.20 × 3,800 hours = <u>£8,360</u>

✓ Solution 15

	£
Actual overhead incurred	280,000
Under-absorbed overhead	20,000
Overhead absorbed	260,000

Overhead absorption rate per machine hour = £260,000/40,000 = £6.50

✓ Solution 16

Required annual profit = £435,000 × 20% = £87,000

Profit as a percentage of total cost = £87,000/£580,000 = 15%

Required cost-plus selling price = £32 + (15% × £32) = £36.80

✓ Solution 17

Number of units, labour hours and machine hours can all be used as a measure of pre-determined absorption rates. A rate per unit is only valid if every unit of output is identical.

So D.

✓ Solution 18

The best description of contribution is sales value less variable cost of sales, which is used in marginal costing.

So B.

✓ Solution 19

$$\frac{\text{Contribution}}{\text{Sales}} = \frac{£4}{£10} = 40\%$$

So C.

✓ Solution 20

$$\frac{\text{Fixed cost}}{\text{C/S ratio}} = \frac{£2,500}{0.4}$$

= £6,250 – if selling price is £10 then the break-even unit figure is 625 units.

So C.

✓ Solution 21

Margin of safety:

= Budgeted sales − Break-even sales
    ─────────────────────────────────
              Budgeted sales

= £10,000 − £6,250 = 0.375
    ─────────────────
         £10,000

or 37.5%.

So B.

✓ Solution 22

$$\frac{\text{Profit target} + \text{Fixed costs}}{\text{c/s radio}} = \frac{£5,000 + £2,500}{0.40}$$

= £18,750.

So C.

✓ Solution 23

Gross profit margin is based on the selling price so, if selling price is £100 and unit cost is £40, the profit is £60 or 60%. Mark-up is based on the unit cost, so a unit cost of £40 which is selling for £100 is a mark-up of 1.5 or 150%.

So A.

✓ Solution 24

Solution 24

The breakeven point on a traditional breakeven chart is where the total cost line and the sales revenue line intersect. This eliminates options A and B.

The breakeven point on a profit-volume chart is where the profit line cuts the horizontal (activity) axis, at zero profit or loss.

So C.

✓ Solution 25

The profit line will cut the vertical axis at $y = -£30,000$. This is the loss at zero activity, which is equal to the fixed cost.

✓ Solution 26

Labour hours required for maximum demand: Hours

Product E 380 units × 0.5 hr	190
Product F 520 units × 1.5 hr	780
Product G 240 units × 1 hr	240
	1,210

Since 1,300 hours are available, labour is not a limiting factor.

Material required for maximum demand: Kg

    Product E 380 units × 1.5 kg   570
    Product F 520 units × 1.25 kg   650
    Product G 240 units × 2 kg   480
                                             1,700

Since only 1,450 kg is available, material supply is a limiting factor.

So B.

✓ Solution 27

Product	X	Y	Z
Contribution per unit	£24	£25	£30
Skilled labour per unit	0.40	0.50	0.75
Contribution per key factor	£60	£50	£40
Rank	1	2	3
Maximum demand	5,000	5,000	2,000
Production	5,000	3,200	–
Labour hours	2,000	1,600	–

So C.

✓ Solution 28

A standard based on last period's actuals or the average of some previous period is known as an historical standard.

So D.

✓ Solution 29

                               hours

Product F – 5,100 × $\frac{6}{60}$ 510

Product C – 2,520 × $\frac{10}{60}$ 420

Product A – 3,150 × $\frac{12}{60}$ 630
                                   1,560

= 120% of budget

so 1,560 × $\frac{100}{120}$ = 1,300 standard hours

So C.

✅ Solution 30

Budgeted labour cost per standard hour:

$$= \frac{\text{Budgeted cost}}{\text{Budgeted standard hour}} = \frac{£2,080}{1,300}$$

$$= £1.60.$$

So C.

✅ Solution 31

Materials price variance:

	£
26,400 × £13 =	343,200
Actual	336,600
Favourable	£6,600

Materials usage variance:

		£
Should have used :	12,000 × 2 × £13	= 312,000
Did use	26,400 × £13	= 343,200

£31,200 Adverse.

So A.

✅ Solution 32

Labour rate:

	£
40,200 × £4	160,800
Actual	168,840
Adverse	£8,040

Labour efficiency:

		£
Should have taken:	12,000 × 3.3 × £4	= 158,400
Did take:	40,200 × £4	= 160,800

£2,400 Adverse

So A.

✅ Solution 33

The sales price variance for the period was £69,000 adverse

46,000 units should sell for (× £34)	1,564,000
But did sell for	1,495,000
Sales price variance	69,000 adverse

✓ Solution 34

The sales volume contribution variance for the period was £14,000 favourable

	Units	
Budgeted sales volume	45,000	
Actual sales volume	46,000	
Sales volume variance in units	1,000	favourable
x standard contribution per unit	£14	
Sales volume contribution variance	£14,000	favourable

✓ Solution 35

Production overhead is collected in the overhead control account during the period. From there it is absorbed as a debit in the work in progress account, using a predetermined overhead absorption rate.

DR WIP control account
CR overhead control account.

So A.

✓ Solution 36

Normal loss = 20% × 5,000 kg = 1,000 kg
Value = 1,000 kg × 30p = £300.

So A.

✓ Solution 37

Abnormal loss = 1,200 − 1,000 = 200 kg

$$\text{Cost per unit} = \frac{\text{Process costs} - \text{normal loss scrap value}}{\text{Input} - \text{normal loss}}$$

$$= \frac{£(5,000 \times 0.5) + £800 + (200\% \times £800) - £300}{5,000 - 1,000}$$

$$= \frac{£4,600}{4,000} = £1.15 \times 200 \text{ kg} = £230$$

So C.

✓ Solution 38

Value = 3,800 kg × £1.15 = £4,370.

So B.

✓ Solution 39

Flow of units

Input = Output + Closing WIP + Normal loss + Abnormal loss

10,000 = 8,000 + 900 + 10% (10,000) + 100 (bal)

Equivalent units

	Output	Abnormal loss	Closing WIP	Total
Materials	8,000	100	900 (100%)	9,000
Labour and overheads	8,000	100	675 (75%)	8,775

Costs per EU:

Materials $\quad\quad\quad\quad\quad \dfrac{£40,500}{9,000} = £4.50$

Labour and overheads $\quad \dfrac{£5,616 \times 1.5}{8,775} = £0.96$

$\quad\quad\quad\quad\quad\quad\quad\quad\quad\quad\quad\quad £5.46$

Abnormal loss value = 100 × £5.46 = £546.

So D.

✓ Solution 40

Output value = 8,000 × £5.46 = £43,680.

So C.

✓ Solution 41

Closing WIP value:

	£
900 × £4.50	4,050
675 × £0.96	648
	4,698

So B.

✓ Solution 42

Materials purchased specifically for the job, or drawn from inventory, direct wages and direct materials would all be shown on a job cost sheet.

So D.

✓ Solution 43

£50 × 100/60 = £83.33

So B.

✓ Solution 44

Senior	86 hours at £20	£1,720
Junior	220 hours at £15	£3,300
Overheads	306 hours at £12.50	£3,825
Total cost		£8,845
Mark-up	(40%)	£3,538
Selling price		**£12,383**

So D.

✓ Solution 45

Senior	750 hours at £20	£15,000
Junior	2,250 hours at £15	£33,750
Overheads	3,000 hours at £12.50	£37,500
Total cost		£86,250
Mark-up	(40%)	£34,500

So A.

✓ Solution 46

The price to be quoted for job no.387 is £2,600

The profit is expressed as a percentage of the selling price.

Therefore selling price = £2,080/0.8 = £2,600

✓ Solution 47

Value certified = £1.3m
Cost of work certified = £1m

National profit £300,000

$$£300,000 \times \frac{\text{Cash received}}{\text{Value certified}}$$

$$= £300,000 \times \frac{£1.2m}{£1.3m}$$

= £276,923.

So B.

✓ Solution 48

Budgeted production of product X during February is <u>566</u> units.

	Units
Required for budgeted sales	560
Plus closing inventory (20% × 590 units)	118
	678
Less opening inventory (20% × 560 units)	(112)
Budgeted production volume	566

✓ Solution 49

The budget cost allowance for maintenance costs for the latest period, when 8,427 maintenance hours were worked, is £214,394

Hours	£
8,520	216,440
8,300	211,600
220	4,840

Variable maintenance cost per hour = £4,840/220 = £22

Fixed maintenance cost = £216,440 − (8,520 hours × £22) = £29,000

Budget cost allowance for 8,427 hours = £29,000 + (8,427 × £22) = £214,394

✓ Solution 50

The receipts from customers in March (to the nearest £) are budgeted to be £69,620

	£
20% received in cash = 20% × £66,200	13,240.00
Credit sales from February (80% × 70% × 98% × £72,900)	40,007.52
Credit sales from January (80% × 27% × £75,800)	16,372.80
Total receipts from customers	69,620.32

Mock Assessment 3

Certificate in Business Accounting
Fundamentals of Management Accounting

You are allowed two hours to complete this assessment.

The assessment contains 50 questions.

All questions are compulsory.

Do not turn the page until you are ready to attempt the assessment under timed conditions.

Mock Assessment Questions

Question 1

A unit of product or service in relation to which costs are ascertained is known as a:

(A) Cost unit
(B) Cost centre
(C) Both A and B
(D) Neither A nor B

Question 2

Prime cost is:

(A) The first cost involved in the production process
(B) The material cost of a product
(C) The labour cost of a product
(D) The total of direct costs

The following information relates to Questions 3 and 4.

The overhead expenses of a company are coded using a six digit coding system. These are based on the cost centre and the type of expense incurred.

Cost Centre	Code No.	Expenses	Code No.
Sales	101	Wages (Stores)	401
Finance	102	Commission Sales	402
Manufacturing	103	Interest Paid	403
Stores	104	Goods Inwards	404

Question 3

The coding for wages in the stores would be:

(A) 104   401
(B) 401   104
(C) 103   401
(D) 404   102

Question 4

The coding for interest paid by the finance department is:

(A) 102   401
(B) 102   403
(C) 403   102
(D) 101   401

Question 5

The information below shows the number of calls made and the monthly telephone bill for the first quarter of last year:

Month	No. of Calls	Cost
January	400	£2,000
February	600	£2,800
March	900	£4,000

Using the high-low method, what was the fixed cost of the line rental each month?

(A) £200
(B) £300
(C) £400
(D) £500

Question 6

During a time of rising prices, which statement is consistent with a first in, first out (FIFO) system of stock control?

(A) Product costs are overstated and profits understated
(B) Product costs are overstated and profits overstated
(C) Product costs are understated and profits understated
(D) Product costs are understated and profits overstated

Questions 7 and 8 are based on the following information:

Receipts and issues of part number JS100 for the month of April are as follows:

	Receipts units	Total value £	Issues units
3 April	2,000	12,000	
7 April	3,000	19,800	
11 April	2,000	16,000	
16 April			4,000
24 April	3,000	21,000	
30 April			5,000

Opening stocks of part number JS100 were 1,000 units, valued at £5,600.

Question 7

Using a FIFO method of stock valuation, the cost of the issued parts in the month was:

(A) £60,400
(B) £60,800
(C) £61,800
(D) £62,200

Question 8

Using a LIFO method of stock valuation, the cost of the issued parts in the month was:

(A) £61,800
(B) £62,200
(C) £62,800
(D) £66,200

Question 9

Which of the following will result in an under absorption of overheads?

(A) Actual overhead is higher than budgeted overhead
(B) Actual production is below budgeted production
(C) Actual overhead is higher than absorbed overhead
(D) Budgeted overhead is higher than actual overhead

Question 10

The following data relate to two output levels of a department:

Machine hours	17,000	18,500
Overheads	£246,500	£251,750

The variable overhead rate per hour is £3.50.

The amount of fixed overheads is:

(A) £5,250
(B) £59,500
(C) £187,000
(D) £246,500

Question 11

A company absorbs overheads on machine hours which were budgeted at 11,250 with overheads of £258,750. Actual results were 10,980 hours with overheads of £254,692.

Overheads were:

(A) Under absorbed by £2,152
(B) Over absorbed by £4,058
(C) Under absorbed by £4,058
(D) Over absorbed by £2,152

Questions 12 and 13 are based on the following information:

A product has an operating statement for the sales of 1,000 units:

	£
Sales	10,000
Variable Costs	6,000
Fixed Costs	2,500

Question 12

The contribution to sales ratio is:

(A) 15%
(B) 25%
(C) 40%
(D) Impossible to determine

Question 13

The margin of safety is:

A) 15%
(B) 25%
(C) 37.5%
(D) 40%

Question 14

H Ltd manufactures and sells two products – J and K. Annual sales are expected to be in the ratio of J:1 K:3. Total annual sales are planned to be £420,000. Product J has a contribution to sales ratio of 40% whereas that of product K is 50%. Annual fixed costs are estimated to be £120,000.

The budgeted break-even sales value (to the nearest £1,000) is:

(A) £196,000
(B) £200,000
(C) £253,000
(D) £255,000

Question 15

Z Ltd manufactures three products, the selling price and cost details of which are given below:

	Product X £	Product Y £	Product Z £
Selling price per unit	75	95	95
Costs per unit:			
Direct materials (£5/kg)	10	5	15
Direct labour (£4/hour)	16	24	20
Variable overhead	8	12	10
Fixed overhead	24	36	30

In a period when direct materials are restricted in supply, the most and the least profitable uses of direct materials are:

	Most profitable	Least profitable
(A)	X	Z
(B)	Y	Z
(C)	X	Y
(D)	Z	Y

Question 16

ABC Ltd uses standard costing. It purchases a small component for which the following data are available:

Actual purchase quantity	6,800 units
Standard allowance for actual production	5,440 units
Standard price	85p/unit
Purchase price variance (ADVERSE)	(£544)

What was the actual purchase price per unit?

(A) 75p
(B) 77p
(C) 93p
(D) 95p

Question 17

Which of the following will normally be included in a standard cost card?

(i) Direct materials
(ii) Direct wages
(iii) Variable overhead
(iv) Fixed overhead

(A) (i) only
(B) (i) and (ii)
(C) (i), (ii) and (iii)
(D) (i), (ii), (iii) and (iv)

Question 18

Trim Ltd's materials price variance for the month of January was £1,000 F and the usage variance was £200 F. The standard material usage per unit is 3 kg and the standard material price is £2 per kg. 500 units were produced in the period. Opening stocks of raw materials were 100 kg and closing stocks 300 kg.

Material purchases in the period were:

(A) 1,200 kg
(B) 1,400 kg
(C) 1,600 kg
(D) 1,800 kg

Question 19

T plc uses a standard costing system, with its material stock account being maintained at standard costs. The following details have been extracted from the standard cost card in respect of direct materials:

8 kg @ £0.80/kg = £6.40 per unit

Budgeted production in April 20X9 was 850 units.

The following details relate to actual materials purchased and issued to production during April 20X9 when actual production was 870 units:

Materials purchased	8,200 kg costing £6.888
Materials issued to production	7,150 kg

Which of the following correctly states the material price and usage variances to be reported?

(A) £286 (A) £152 (A)
(B) £286 (A) £280 (A)
(C) £286 (A) £294 (A)
(D) £328 (A) £152 (A)

Question 20

Z plc uses a standard costing system and has the following labour cost standard in relation to one of its products:

4 hours skilled labour @ £6.00 per hour   £24.00

During October 20X9, 3,350 of these products were made which was 150 units less than budgeted. The labour cost incurred was £79,893 and the number of direct labour hours worked was 13,450.

The direct labour variances for the month were:

	Rate	Efficiency
(A)	£804 (F)	£300 (A)
(B)	£804 (F)	£300 (F)
(C)	£807 (F)	£297 (A)
(D)	£807 (F)	£300 (A)

Question 21

In the cost ledger the factory cost of finished production for a period was £873,190. The double entry for this is:

(A) Dr Cost of sales account
    Cr Finished goods control account
(B) Dr Finished goods control account
    Cr Work-in-progress control account
(C) Dr Costing profit and loss account
    Cr Finished goods control account
(D) Dr Work-in-progress control account
    Cr Finished goods control account

Question 22

A firm operates an integrated cost and financial accounting system. The accounting entries for Absorbed Manufacturing Overhead would be:

(A) Dr Overhead control account
    Cr Work-in-progress control account

(B) Dr Finished goods control account
   Cr Overhead control account
(C) Dr Overhead control account
   Cr Finished goods control account
(D) Dr Work-in-progress control account
   Cr Overhead control account

Questions 23 – 25 are based on the information below.

JEDPRINT LTD

Jedprint Ltd specialises in printing advertising leaflets and is in the process of preparing its price list. The most popular requirement is for a folded leaflet made from a single sheet of A4 paper. From past records and budgeted figures, the following data have been estimated for a typical batch of 10,000 leaflets:

Artwork	£65
Machine setting	4 hours @ £22 per hour
Paper	£12.50 per 1,000 sheets
Ink and consumables	£40
Printers' wages	4 hours @ £8 per hour

Note: Printers' wages vary with volume.

General fixed overheads are £15,000 per period during which a total of 600 labour hours are expected to be worked.

The firm wishes to achieve 30% profit on sales.

Question 23

The direct cost of producing 10,000 leaflets was:

(A) £350
(B) £450
(C) £475
(D) £525

Question 24

The profit from selling 10,000 units would be:

(A) £150
(B) £164.16
(C) £175.42
(D) £192.86

Question 25

The selling price is:

(A) £450
(B) £525.25
(C) £602.26
(D) £642.86

Questions 26 – 28 are concerned with the following information about a contract.

	£000
1. Costs incurred to date	2,740
2. Costs estimated to complete contract	3,870
3. Value of work certified to date	3,120
4. Total value of contract	7,250

? Question 26

What is the total expected contract profit?

(A) £600,000
(B) £640,000
(C) £720,000
(D) £760,000

? Question 27

Calculate the attributable profit using costs as a measure of completion:

(A) £202,000
(B) £242,000
(C) £262,000
(D) £262,400

? Question 28

Attributable profit using sales value as a measure of completion is:

(A) £250,000
(B) £276,490
(C) £640,000
(D) £720,000

Questions 29 – 30 are based on the following data.

Input	5,000 kg
Normal loss	5%
Process costs	£16,500
Actual output	4,600 kg

Losses are sold for £2.35 per kg.

? Question 29

The scrap value of the normal loss was:

(A) £587.50
(B) £625.50
(C) £631.48
(D) £700.00

Question 30

The net cost of the abnormal loss was:

(A) £100
(B) £150
(C) £587.50
(D) £15,912.50

Question 31

A process produces two joint products A and B. During the month of December, the process costs attributed to complete output amounted to £122,500. Output of X and Y for the period was:

X	3 tonnes
Y	4 tonnes

The cost attributed to product X using the weight basis of apportionment was:

(A) £45,750
(B) £50,150
(C) £51,250
(D) £52,500

The following information relates to questions 32, 33 and 34.

A product is manufactured as a result of two processes, 1 and 2. Details of process 2 for the latest period were as follows:

Materials transferred from process 1	10,000 kg valued at £40,800
Labour and overhead costs	£8,4224
Output transferred to finished goods	8,000 kg
Closing work-in-progress	900 kg

Normal loss is 10% of input and losses have a scrap value of £0.30 per kg.

Closing work-in-progress is 100% complete for material, and 75% complete for labour and overheads.

Question 32

The value of the output for the period was £ (to the nearest £).

Question 33

The value of abnormal loss for the period was £ (to the nearest £).

Question 34

The value of the closing work-in-progress for the period was £ (to the nearest £).

Question 35

Which of the following are characteristics of service costing?

(i) High levels of indirect costs as a proportion of total costs
(ii) Use of composite cost units
(iii) Use of equivalent units

(A) (i) only
(B) (i) and (ii) only
(C) (ii) only
(D) (ii) and (iii) only

Question 36

Calculate the most appropriate unit cost for a distribution company based on the following data:

1. Miles travelled   500,000
2. Tonnes carried   2,500
3. No. of drivers   25
4. Hours worked by drivers 37,500
5. Tonne miles carried   375,000
6. Costs incurred   £500,000

(A) £1.25
(B) £1.33
(C) £1.50
(D) £1.75

Question 37

Which of the following are objectives of budgeting?

(i) Resource allocation
(ii) Expansion
(iii) Communication
(iv) Co-ordination

(A) (i), (ii)
(B) (i), (ii), (iii)
(C) (i), (iii), (iv)
(D) (i), (ii), (iii), (iv)

Questions 38 – 40 are based on the following information.

JK Ltd has recently completed its sales forecasts for the year to 31st December 20X9. It expects to sell two products – J and K – at prices of £135 and £145 each respectively.

Sales demand is expected to be:

    J   10,000 units
    K   6,000 units

Both products use the same raw materials and skilled labour but in different quantities per unit:

	J	K
Material X	10 kgs	6 kgs
Material Y	4 kgs	8 kgs
Skilled labour	6 hours	4 hours

The prices expected during 20X9 for the raw materials are:

| Material X | £1.50 per kg |
| Material Y | £4.00 per kg |

The skilled labour rate is expected to be £6.00 per hour.

Stocks of raw materials and finished goods on 1st January 20X9 are expected to be:

Material X	400 kgs @ £1.20 per kg
Material Y	200 kgs @ £3.00 per kg
J	600 units @ £70.00 each
K	800 units @ £60.00 each

All stocks are to be reduced by 15% from their opening levels by the end of 20X9 and are valued using the FIFO method.

The company uses absorption costing, and production overhead costs are expected to be:

| Variable | £2.00 per skilled labour hour |
| Fixed | £315,900 per annum |

Question 38

The production (in units) of product J is:

(A) 510
(B) 600
(C) 9,910
(D) 10,000

Question 39

The amount spent on materials X and Y for the period were:

(A) £201,480
(B) £203,420
(C) £205,740
(D) £209,220

Question 40

The unit value of finished closing stocks of K were:

(A) £50,641
(B) £55,247
(C) £58,375
(D) £60,003

Question 41

Dougal is preparing a cash budget for July. His credit sales are:

		£
April	(actual)	80,000
May	(actual)	60,000
June	(actual)	40,000
July	(estimated)	50,000

His recent debt collection experience has been as follows:

Current month's sales	20%
Prior month's sales	60%
Sales two months prior	10%
Cash discounts taken	5%
Bad debts	5%

How much may Dougal expect to collect from debtors during July?

(A) £48,000
(B) £42,000
(C) £40,000
(D) £36,000

Question 42

Macnamara is preparing a cash budget for July. His credit sales are:

		£
April	(actual)	40,000
May	(actual)	30,000
June	(actual)	20,000
July	(estimated)	25,000

His recent debt collection experience has been as follows:

Current month's sales	20%
Prior month's sales	65%
Sales two months prior	10%
Cash discounts taken	2.5%
Bad debts	2.5%

How much may Macnamara expect to collect from debtors during July?

(A) £19,000
(B) £20,000
(C) £21,000
(D) £24,000

Question 43

The following details have been extracted from the debtor collection records of C Ltd:

Invoices paid in the month after sale	60%
Invoices paid in the second month after sale	25%
Invoices paid in the third month after sale	12%
Bad debts	3%

Invoices are issued on the last day of each month.

Customers paying in the month after sale are entitled to deduct a 2% settlement discount.

Credit sales values for June to September 20X9 are budgeted as follows:

June	July	August	September
£35,000	£40,000	£60,000	£45,000

The amount budgeted to be received from credit sales in September 20X9 is:

(A) £47,280
(B) £47,680
(C) £48,850
(D) £49,480

Question 44

A master budget comprises:

(A) The budgeted profit and loss account
(B) The budgeted cashflow, budgeted profit and loss account and budgeted balanced sheet
(C) The budgeted cashflow
(D) The capital expenditure budget

Question 45

When preparing a production budget, the quantity to be produced equals:

(A) Sales quantity + opening stock + closing stock
(B) Sales quantity − opening stock + closing stock
(C) Sales quantity − opening stock − closing stock
(D) Sales quantity + opening stock − closing stock

Question 46

A budget which recognises different cost behaviour patterns is designed to change as volume of activity changes is known as:

(A) A Flexible Budget
(B) A Flexed Budget
(C) A Fixed Budget
(D) None of the above

Questions 47 – 49 are based on the following data.

	Budget	Actual
Production	10,000 units	9750
Direct labour	£40,000	£40,250
Variable overhead	£50,000	£47,500
Depreciation	£20,000	£20,000

Question 47

The direct labour variance was:

(A) £1,250 A
(B) £1,250 F
(C) £2,500 A
(D) £2,500 F

Question 48

The variable overhead variance was:

(A) £1,250 A
(B) £1,250 F
(C) £2,500 A
(D) £2,500 F

Question 49

If volume variance is £7,500 adverse, and expenditure is £3,100 favourable, then the total variance is:

(A) £4,400 A
(B) £7,500 A
(C) £3,100 F
(D) £4,400 F

Question 50

Which of the following are features of the service industry?

(i) Intangibility
(ii) Heterogeneity
(iii) Simultaneous production and consumption
(iv) Perishability

(A) (i) only
(B) (i) and (ii)
(C) (i), (ii) and (iii)
(D) (i), (ii), (iii) and (iv)

Mock Assessment 3 – Solutions

✅ Solution 1

A cost unit is a unit of product or service in relation to which costs are ascertained.

A cost centre is a production or service location, function activity or item of equipment for which costs are accumulated.

So A.

✅ Solution 2

Prime Cost is Direct Materials, Direct Labour and Direct Expenses.

So D.

✅ Solution 3

104   401

So A.

✅ Solution 4

102   403

So B.

✅ Solution 5

	Units	Cost
Highest month	900	4,000
Lowest month	400	2,000
	500	2,000

Additional cost = $\frac{£2,000}{500}$ = £4 per unit

So taking either higher or lower number:

Higher 900 × £4 = £3,600   Fixed Cost = £400
Lower 4,500 × £4 = £1,600   Fixed Cost = £400

So C.

✅ Solution 6

Product costs are understated and profits are overstated. FIFO uses the oldest items in the inventory.

So D.

✓ Solution 7

Value of parts issued using FIFO:

16th April

		£
1,000 @ £5.60		5,600
2,000 @ £6.00		12,000
1,000 @ £6.60		6,600
		24,200

30th April

		£
2,000 @ £6.60		13,200
2,000 @ £8.00		16,000
1,000 @ £7.00		7,000
		36,200

Total value of parts issued £60,400.

So A.

✓ Solution 8

Value of parts issued using LIFO:

16th April

		£
2,000 × £8.00		16,000
2,000 × £6.60		13,200
		29,200

30th April

		£
3,000 @ £7.00		21,000
1,000 @ £6.60		6,600
1,000 @ £6.00		6,000
		33,600

Total value of parts issued £62,800.

So C.

✓ Solution 9

If actual production is below budgeted production, fixed overheads are spread over fewer units.

So B.

✓ Solution 10

	£
Total Cost of 17,000 hours	246,500
Variable Cost of 17,000 hours (× £3.50)	59,500
Balance Fixed Cost	187,000

So C.

✓ Solution 11

Overhead absorption rate

$$= \frac{£258,750}{11,250} = £23 \text{ per hour}$$

Actual overheads	£254,692
10,980 × 23 =	£252,540
	£2,152

under absorbed by £2,152.

So A.

✓ Solution 12

Contribution to Sales Ratio:

Sales	£10,000
Variable Cost	£6,000
Contribution	£4,000

Contribution to sales = $\frac{£4,000}{£10,000}$ = 40%

So C.

✓ Solution 13

Margin of safety is the difference between budgeted sales volume and break-even sales volume:

$$\frac{\text{Fixed Costs}}{\text{Contribution}} = \frac{2,500}{.4}$$

Break-even sales value £6,250
Break-even sales volume £625 units

1,000 − 625 = 375

$\frac{375}{1000}$ = 37.5%

So C.

✓ Solution 14

Weighted Average C/S Ratio:

$$\frac{(1 \times 40\%) + (3 \times 50\%)}{4} = 47.5\%$$

Break-even $\dfrac{\text{Fixed Costs}}{\text{C/S Sales}}$ $\dfrac{£120,000}{0.475}$

= 252,632.

So C.

✓ Solution 15

Product	X	Y	Z
Contribution	41	54	50
Materials	2	1	3
Contribution per LF	£20.50	£54	£16.66
Banking	2	1	3

So B.

✓ Solution 16

Actual purchases at standard price:

6,800 × 85p	£5,780
Adverse price variance	£544
Actual purchases at actual price	£6,324

$\dfrac{£6,324}{£6,800} = 93p.$

So C.

✓ Solution 17

Direct Materials, Direct Wages, Variable Overhead and Fixed Overhead are all included in a standard cost card.

So D.

✓ Solution 18

Standard quantity used	500 × 3 = £1,500	
Usage variance	100	Favourable
Materials used	1,400	
Opening stock	(100)	
Closing stock	300	
	1,600	

So C.

✅ Solution 19

Price variance:

		£
8,200 kg should cost £0.80/kg	=	6,560
Actual cost	=	6,888
		328 (A)

Usage variance:

870 units should use 8 kg each	=	6,960 kg
Actual usage	=	7,150 kg
		190 kg
190 kg @ £0.80/kg	=	£152 kg

So D.

✅ Solution 20

Rate variance:

	£
Standard cost of actual hours (13,450 × £6)	80,700
Actual cost	79,893
	807 (F)

Efficiency variance:

Standard hours produced (3,350 × 4)		13,400
Actual hours		13,450
Extra hours		50 (A)
Variance =	50 × £6 =	£300 (A)

So D.

✅ Solution 21

DR Finished Goods Control Account
CR Work-in-Progress Account

So. B.

✅ Solution 22

In a cost accounting system, the absorption of manufacturing overhead represents a cost to be charged for work-in-progress with the corresponding bookkeeping entry being a credit to the overhead control account.

So D.

✓ Solution 23

Direct cost of producing 10,000 leaflets:

	£
Artwork	65
Machine setting	88
Paper	125
Ink	40
Wages	32
	350

So A.

✓ Solution 24

Profit from selling 10,000 units:

Direct Cost	350
Overheads	100
Total Cost	450

Profit = $\frac{30}{70} \times 450 = 192.86$

So D.

✓ Solution 25

Selling Price =	Total Cost	450
×	Profit	192.86
		642.86

So D.

✓ Solution 26

Expected Contract Profit:

	£000
Contract value	7,250
Costs incurred	(2,740)
Costs to complete	(3,870)
Expected profit	640

So B.

✓ Solution 27

Using Costs

$$\frac{2,740}{6,610} \times 640,000 = 262,400$$

So D.

✅ Solution 28

$$\frac{\text{Value Certified}}{\text{Total Value}} = \frac{3,120}{7,250} \times 640,000$$

= 276,490.

So B.

✅ Solution 29

Normal loss = 250 kg
Scrap value = 250 × £2.35 = £587.50.

So A.

✅ Solution 30

Expected Output	2,750 kg
Actual Output	2,600 kg
Volume of abnormal loss	150 kg

Cost per unit £3.35 − Scrap value of normal loss £2.15,
So 150 × £1.00 = £150.00.

So B.

✅ Solution 31

Cost attributed to Product X:

$\frac{3}{7} \times £122,500 = £52,500$

So D.

✅ Solution 32

STEP 1:

STATEMENT OF EQUIVALENT UNITS

	Total Units		Materials Units		Labour & Overhead Units
Completed output	8,000	(100%)	8,000	(100%)	8,000
Normal loss	1,000	(0%)	-	(0%)	-
Abnormal loss	100	(100%)	100	(100%)	100
Closing WIP	900	(100%)	900	(75%)	675
	10,000		9,000		8,775

STEP 2:

STATEMENT OF COST PER EQUIVALENT UNIT

	Materials	Labour & Overhead
Total costs	*£40,500	£8,424
Equivalent units	9,000	8,775
Cost per equivalent unit	£4.50	£0.96

*£40,800 less scrap value normal loss £300 = £40,500

Total cost per unit = £(4.50 + 0.96)

= £5.46

STATEMENT OF EVALUATION

Output

8,000 kg @ £5.46 = £43,680.

✅ Solution 33

The value of abnormal loss for the period was £546 (to the nearest £)
From question 33, 100 units abnormal loss × £5.46 = £546.

✅ Solution 34

The value of the closing work-in-progress for the period was £4,698 (to the nearest £)
From question 33, costs per equivalent unit are:

Materials	£4.50
Labour and Overhead	£0.96

Evaluation of work-in-progress:

	£
Materials 900 equivalent units × £4.50	4,050
Labour and Overhead 675 equivalent units × £0.96	648
	4,698

✅ Solution 35

Characteristics of Service Costing:

(i) High levels of indirect costs as a proportion of total costs,
e.g. rent for a restaurant. YES
(ii) Use of composite cost units, e.g. tonne mile. YES
(iii) Use of equivalent units. This is used in process costing. NO

So B – (i) and (ii).

✅ Solution 36

The most appropriate cost unit in this example is the tonne mile:

$$\frac{£500,000}{375,000} = £1.33$$

So B.

✅ Solution 37

Resource allocation, communication and co-ordination are all objectives of budgeting, odd one out is expansion.

So C.

✅ Solution 38

Production in units of Product J:

Sales	10,000
Closing stock (85%)	510
Opening stock	600
	9,910

So C.

✅ Solution 39

Amount spent on materials X:

		kg
Required for J	9,910 × 10 kg	99,100
Required for K	5,880 × 6 kg	32,280
Opening stock		(400)
Closing stock		340
		134,320

134 × £1.50 = £201,480.

So A.

✅ Solution 40

Unit value of finished closing stock of K:

		£
Material X	6 × £1.50	9
Material Y	8 × £4.00	32
Direct labour	4 × £6.00	24
Variable overhead	4 × £2.00	8
Fixed overhead (see W1)	4 × £3.81	15.24
	unit cost	88.24

85% of 800 = 680 x £88.24 = £60,003.00

W1:

Fixed overhead absorbed on direct labour hours –

J	9,910 × 6	59,460.00
K	5,880 × 4	23,520.00
		82,980.00

Rate - £315,900 = £3.81
       82,980

So D.

✓ Solution 41

50,000 × 20%	£10,000
40,000 × 60%	£24,000
60,000 × 10%	£6,000
	£40,000

So C.

✓ Solution 42

25,000 × 20%	£5,000
20,000 × 65%	£13,000
30,000 × 10%	£3,000
	£21,000

So C.

✓ Solution 43

60% of August sales less 2% discount:

60,000 × 60% × 98%	£35,280
25% July sales	
£40,000 × 25%	£10,000
12% of June sales	
£35,000 × 12%	£4,200
	£49,480

So D.

✓ Solution 44

A master budget is used to describe the set of summary budgets

So B.

✓ Solution 45

A production budget works in the opposite way to an income statement. To find gross profit, we add opening stock and subtract closing stock. With production we add closing and subtract opening.

So B.

✓ Solution 46

A flexible budget is a budget which by recognising different cost behaviour patterns is designed to change as volume of activity changes.

So A.

✓ Solution 47

Standard cost of direct labour	£4 per unit
9,750 units should have cost	£39,000
9,750 units did cost	£40,250
Direct labour is	£1,250 A

So A.

✓ Solution 48

Variable overhead should be	£5 per unit
Actual production × standard overhead – 9,750 × £5	£48,750
Actual variable overhead	£47,500
	£1,250 F

So B.

✓ Solution 49

Volume	£7,500 A
Expenditure	£3,100 F
	£4,400 A

So A.

✓ Solution 50

INTANGIBILITY – Output takes the form of a performance, e.g. a waiter.
HETEROGENEITY – Standard of service is variable due to human element, e.g. chef.
SIMULTANEOUS PRODUCTION CONSUMPTION – e.g. hairdresser.
PERISHABILITY – Cannot hold stock, e.g. airline seats.

So all are features – Answer D.